To

My mom, Dalia, who taught me that education is a person's most prized possession
My dad, Baruch, who taught me that hard work always pays off
My husband, Itzhak, who empowers me to reach my wildest dreams
My children, Ohad and Gonny, who keep me grounded and unselfish
My mentor, Gania, who equips me with life's intangible necessities

And to the unbelievably brave women in my life who share the journey with me,
and teach me the secrets of the strength and resilience of the female spirit

I love you all deeply.

THE OPPOSITE OF COMFORTABLE

The Unlikely Choices of an Immigrant Career Woman

SHARON NIR

First Published in the United States of America by Viki Press
Published in 2016

www.sharonnir.com

The Library of Congress Control Number: 2015920863

ISBN 978-0-9971430-0-3 (pbk.)
ISBN 978-0-9971430-1-0 (ebook)

FIRST EDITION

Printed in the United States of America

Thank you!

TABLE OF CONTENTS

1

✿

RUNNING LATE

It was a little before 6 am, and my thirteen-month-old baby boy was crying. My husband's side of the bed was empty. His call schedule as a fifth-year general surgery resident was especially demanding. I knew I should get up, but I felt exhausted.

The night before, I had stayed awake until midnight. I was busy drawing sketches for a new promotions screen for the Knowledge Management system I had implemented almost a year ago. A recent survey had indicated the call center customer service representatives were experiencing difficulties using the software to provide instant answers to customers' questions. The telecommunication company I worked for had invested thousands of dollars in the system. I had no intention of letting them down.

Reluctantly, I got out of bed. It was cold. The rooster was crowing from a distance, and our neighbors' dog started barking. Ever since the canine had found his way to the chicken coop, they didn't like each other. After a short, yet epic, match, both sides were left mentally scarred. I thought it was a fantastic validation of the philosophic dilemma of what came first, the chicken or the egg: was it the rooster's early wakeup calls that had provoked the canine's attack, or was it the canine's howls next to the coop that made the rooster fight for his honor? Either way, every morning the symphony of the dog and the rooster played around the same time.

I lifted my son from his crib, kissed him softly, and cradled him in my arms for a few minutes. He calmed down, and I carried him to the kitchen, and while I was half asleep, I warmed up his bottle in the microwave. It was before sunrise and the house was dark. I took my son to my bed, organized the pillows behind me, sat back down, and sniffed his brownish curly hair that smelled warm and sweet, while he was slowly sucking on his bottle. When he had finished eating, I left him in his crib and went to the kitchen. I turned on the coffee machine and listened to my son chattering to himself. His vocabulary consisted of only a couple of words, but he babbled short syllables and mimicked the intonation and rhythm of the language he heard us use. I thought he had started to comprehend a few words like names and everyday objects.

After having a cup of coffee, I changed his diaper, placed him in his rocking chair in front of the TV, and played a Baby Van Gogh videotape. It was by far his favorite tape of the series, but back then, we didn't know the reason. He loved watching the video that presented basic colors: red, orange, yellow, blue, green, and purple through the context of images and emotions. The real-life images were visually attractive, and every time one of Van Gogh's paintings appeared on the screen, he clapped his tiny hands and cheered loudly. I knew I had half an hour to get ready for the busy day ahead.

I was about to leave the house when my phone rang. It was never good news when my phone rang that early in the morning. My employee was on the other end. She sounded anxious. "The marketing department is doing it again. They hold information until the last minute. This time, they haven't informed us about rate changes. We don't have time to correct the numbers in the system. We had to make a hard copy and print it out for the use of the call center representatives. They will have the new rates but will have to calculate the sales tax manually when customers ask for the bottom line. As a result, the calls are expected to take longer than usual, and the overall customer wait time would probably increase to three minutes. Be prepared for a call from the center's director," she alerted me.

Although the Knowledge Management system had been implemented almost nine months ago after a massive organizational change, it was still very hard for the people of different departments to share information. I understood the reason behind this difficulty. Information is the ONLY thing that cannot be taken unwillingly from an individual. In every organization, and the one I worked for was no different, people feel their intellectual property is their competitive advantage that will protect them or provide them with leverage in a time of trouble. Yet organizations must acquire this knowledge, maintain it, and make it available for the entire organization to use. The collective knowledge and its implementation is the source of companies' competitive advantage and leverage among competitors.

As the project manager who was responsible for the design and implementation of a Knowledge Management system, it was my responsibility to reassure employees that sharing their knowledge would not only allow them to perform their job more efficiently but would enable organizational growth from which they would benefit.

I took a deep breath. I wasn't supposed to be at the office until later that day. I had meetings planned at the headquarters of the software development company I had hired to build the system. We needed to decide on a new screen for service promotions.

"Thank you for finding a temporary solution. Please ask the team to withhold other projects, and instead insert the new rates into the system as soon as possible," I said briskly, choosing practicality over criticism.

I checked my watch. It was getting late. Baby Van Gogh's tape had ended, and my son started uncomfortably moving in his chair. I picked him up, keyed the speed dial number for the call center director, and briefed him about the latest development. He wasn't happy to hear that calls were expected to take longer, because the volume of calls had increased in the last few days due to a special holiday sale.

"I promise to add this item to the list of issues we need to discuss in our weekly executive meeting. I know the marketing department should do better; we'll find a way to help them." I attempted to appease him.

Finally, I called my manager and explained the situation. At the same time, my son pushed up against my right hip bone and tried to grab the phone. I placed him on the cold floor, and he started crying. Then I went into another room, quickly reminded my manager that I would be out of the office most of the day, and promised to update her once the new rates were in the system.

Every minute in life was accounted for, but it seemed as if minutes weighed even more in the mornings. I had wanted to avoid the rush hour, but I had to drop off my son at daycare, and I knew I would get stuck in the notorious traffic jam on the freeway on my way to Tel Aviv. I stopped by the daycare center gate. Thankfully, the teacher was outside with a few kids.

"Good morning," she greeted us with a heartfelt smile. "We were about to go inside, come join us." She opened her arms, and my son leaned in. I walked back to the car; my son waved at me, and I blew him a kiss in return.

When I finally entered the office, the meeting had already started, and I joined it just in time for my screen design presentation. Two hours later, we finished the meeting and went to the company's auditorium to listen to a lecture about The Magic of Repositioning.

I knew the speaker from my early days in the industry. Dr. S was an entrepreneur and managing director of an innovative book publishing startup dealing with publishing books through the Internet. She was also a consultant to many leading companies in Israel, focusing on the implementation of Knowledge Management systems. Both digital books and Knowledge Management were relatively new-to-the-market business ventures, but Dr. S never let doubt control her agenda. I admired her determination and dedication to the cause and immediately after I had been recruited by the telecommunication company, I hired her as my consultant. She had given me direction and advised me to focus on the human aspect and its significant contribution to the success or failure of the project. I hadn't spoken to her for the last year, and reposition was a topic I was interested in for a good reason.

Dr. S gave a great lecture about the options that companies have when they experience declining performance due to major shifts in consumers' preferences or needs. She explained firms have two choices: exit the market, or use tactics to extend their brand or product lifecycle, also known as repositioning.

The bottom line of repositioning is to reinvent oneself, and companies should swallow their pride and look inside and out, in order to figure out a way to realign their offerings to customers' needs and wants, and by doing that, reclaim a competitive advantage and regain growth. I thought about the company I worked for. If my organization experienced a decline in sales would it have the courage, and both tangible and intangible resources, to go through a repositioning process? I figured that only companies with great personality would succeed because "personality goes a long way" as Jules Winnfield, the hitman who found god in the excellent movie *Pulp Fiction*, insightfully said.

Repositioning is not about obliterating the past and discounting the old glory. It is about reviving, rejuvenating, and regenerating what you already have in a way that will be aligned with the new environmental conditions. It is about going back to where it all started and beginning anew. What about me as a manager, an employee, an individual would I be able to reposition myself if I needed to? Would I have the courage and the ability to reinvent myself?

I stared at the brainy quotes calendar that hung on the wall across the room. It was February 27, 2001, and the month's quote was by Albert Einstein who said, "Only a life lived for others is a life worthwhile." At that point in time, I had no clue how profound, insightful, and truthful that sentence was.

At the end of the lecture, I shared lunch with Dr. S, and she said other companies had started to express an interest in Knowledge Management systems. The system I had designed and implemented for the call center was the second of its kind in Israel. She asked if I was ready to move to my next project.

I wasn't. I told her that the system had been active for nine months and still had a long way to go. There were new screens for me to design, processes to learn, and knowledge-sharing culture to establish. What I didn't tell her was that I had been procrastinating on a decision that could influence my entire life.

After lunch, I called the office. My team informed me they had just finished updating the new rates. They also said there was an interface glitch in another place in the system. I promised to take care of it. I emailed my manager the crisis was over and joined the development team for what was supposed to be a two-hour session of design and development.

I hadn't noticed it was getting late. I had to leave the development team by 4:30 pm and make it back to my office. I had planned to meet with my team. I knew they had had some problems with sorting information, and I wanted to learn more about their challenges. It was already 4:45 pm. I dug my phone out of my briefcase and opened it. There were ten unanswered calls. I skimmed through them and realized my husband had called a few times. I clicked my voice mail and listened to his first message.

He said that he remembered it was his responsibility to pick up our son from daycare, but there had been another suicide bombing attack on a northbound 6 bus at the French Hill junction in Jerusalem. Many people had been injured, and paramedics had transported the wounded to all three major hospitals in town. He needed to cover the trauma unit and wasn't sure he would be able to make it back on time.

In the second message, he said that the hospital had received the majority of the injured, and he would not come home that night. He was sorry. He wanted me to kiss our son for him. I got into my car and rushed to the daycare, but I was late again.

2

⚜

LIFE TAKES AN UNEXPECTED TURN

From childhood, I was taught to remain calm and composed in potentially hostile situations. My mom hoped that by the time I reached adulthood, her teaching would sink in and I would demonstrate an ability to recover quickly from most of the unfortunate situations that life threw at me. She always said that when someone was calm, they could think and respond rationally to a challenging situation. But I assume she never considered a situation in which my whole life was about to change. In that case, would she think it is possible to stay calm? And what would she consider a rational response?

A month earlier, my husband had been selected for a two-year, multi-organ transplantation fellowship at Mount Sinai Hospital in New York. In medicine, specialties are a significant part of diagnosis and treatment, and surgeons tend to choose a specialty according to their interest, financial objectives, or market demand. The transplant fellowship was aligned with my husband's interest as a few years before we met, he spent one year of his residency at Mount Sinai Hospital in New York as part of the traditional student exchange program employed by the hospital where he worked. During that year, he was exposed to transplantation surgery and was captivated by the challenging, technical, and astonishing nature of this field.

On a Saturday morning, we were sitting on the couch, having coffee; he sat with his laptop open on his lap, while I read the newspaper, and our son was playing on the carpet next to us.

Suddenly, my husband pushed his computer to the side and bounced to his feet, spilling coffee onto the carpet. Covering his mouth with his hand, he called out, "Wow," while my son and I stared at him in bewilderment.

"Wow what?" I asked when I came back from the kitchen with a paper towel in hand. During the minute I was gone, his facial expression had shifted from ecstatic to gloomy.

"I was accepted to the fellowship program in New York," he said without looking at me.

That statement was my cue to congratulate him on his great achievement, but I couldn't.

When he had applied for a transplantation fellowship at one of the most active transplantation centers in the world, I knew that if he were selected, it would be a lifetime opportunity, one that was not open to every surgeon and one that would yield both professional growth and competitive advantage. I realized that it would have been foolish to forego this opportunity.

What's more, as his wife and someone who cared for him deeply, I didn't want him to reject an option that would affect his entire future. I could identify with the situation, because we had a lot in common. We were both ambitious, target-oriented, motivated individuals that were unwilling to settle for less than what we believed was possible for us to achieve. People with those characteristics cannot peacefully walk away from a chance to reach their dreams. Yet, I believed that although we were married, we were two individuals with different needs, aspirations, and hopes for the future.

To be honest, I thought the likelihood that he would be accepted to the fellowship was slim due to the program's competitive nature, so I had promised myself not to bring up my point of view until we knew the answer. When he was accepted, it was my time to speak up.

To work in the United States, my husband had to receive a visa. It was widely known that not all visas are created equal, and they certainly did not promise liberty and the pursuit of happiness. Some of them could lead to years of genuine misery. My husband was expected to receive a J-1 visa, which was an exchange visitor, non-immigrant visa. It allowed an individual to participate in a work-and-study-based exchange visitor program. Unlike other visas, such as the H or the O visa, the individual had to leave the United States immediately after the program ended and return to the country of last residence for two years before applying for any other visa or for a non-immigrant status.

The implications of the fellowship were well-defined. I would have to leave my career, my home, my family and friends, and my country, with the hope I could get everything back upon my return. If I wished to keep our family together, I would have to freeze my life for two years and thaw it out two years later. "I'm so proud of you! This is terrific!" I finally said after a few moments of silence.

I did not tell him then that I was also proud of my accomplishments, and that I felt my work on my project wasn't done yet. I might be able to find a job in my field in New York, but there was a good chance companies would not hire a project manager with an expiration date.

"You only have two years in New York, and it'll take time for me to find a job," I said solemnly.

My husband looked back at me and met the displeased expression that was flashing across my face. He inhaled deeply and rationally explained, "There are two options available; both are far from perfect for you. The first option is that you'll join me in New York and try to find a job for the two years or maybe decide to take some time off. The second is that you'll stay here, follow your career path, and become a single mother for two years. It's your decision to make. I cannot imagine what it would be like if you both stayed behind. There's time to think about it."

He had a way of stripping away any illusions I might have, and serving me the truth on a clear platter so I could see it from each and every angle. Sometimes this approach helped me make the right decision. Other times I really hated it, especially when I wanted to daydream or fantasize about a future in which things fell into place and life was comfortable and secure. I knew then if I said what I wanted to say, we would end up trapped in a huge fight, because I was angry, frustrated, and terribly annoyed. I wasn't upset with him as much as I was upset about the situation.

It's a professional takeover. In business, a takeover is usually a hostile situation when a person or a company ousts a firm's management and takes control of the company. In my case, my career was about to be ousted by my husband's career, not to mention our family. I remembered in hostile situations I had been advised to remain calm and composed, but at that moment, my primitive instincts came to the fore, and my lessons of restraint were unequal to the challenge, and I started freaking-out.

My son had gotten bored playing with his bricks and took a few wobbly steps towards me, pointing outside with his finger. It was great timing: I needed to leave the house and walk. Every time I had to process information or think about a solution, I would take a walk.

We lived in Kfar Sirkin, a scenic village located in the center of Israel east of Tel Aviv. It was surrounded by lush Eucalyptus trees, old quaking Aspens, and orchards with the sweetest oranges you can find. We had moved there a few months before our son was born, because it was between Jerusalem, where my husband worked, and Tel Aviv/ Petach-Tikva, where I worked. I loved how quiet and peaceful the small village was. After a frantic day of work, I enjoyed coming back to this little piece of heaven.

I dressed my son in warm clothes, took his water bottle, placed him in his stroller, and started walking. *Years ago, an offer to live for two years in New York City would have been a dream come true.* I remembered the first time I had traveled to the United States in 1994. My boyfriend and I had spent a month traveling up and down the east coast. The city was the port between every trip, whether we went north or south, and each time I couldn't wait to get back to Manhattan. It was love at first sight, and after returning home to Israel from that trip, I felt a constant longing, and I knew one day I would return. I didn't know how, or what might happen that would allow me to live there, but I knew I would return.

Six years after that visit, the boyfriend and travels had been replaced by a husband, a baby, and a demanding career. I didn't think as often about living in New York. But now my husband had accepted a fellowship, and my desire to live in the city became possible. However, my early twenties' romantic plan to live abroad seemed daunting, when I realized what I would have to leave behind.

I was the project manager and analyst of a new Knowledge Management system at the largest telecommunication firm in Israel. I was responsible for every single aspect of the product, from the analysis stage to the design, quality assurance, final production, and implementation throughout the organization.

Knowledge Management was a relatively new concept, and the organization had to go through a transformation, which included knowledge sharing between departments in a way that had never been done before. Not only was I needed to manage the technical aspects of the system, I also had to find my inner psychologist to handle the human factor embedded in the project. Dealing with people was much more challenging than dealing with the actual project at hand, and my job was to make the system essential to the employees, as much as it was to the organization. I understood collaboration among the organizational departments was vital, and I had worked hard to make colleagues understand the concept and engage in the process.

The resistance to the idea of the system had initiated immediately after I was employed and introduced to the different departments. The call center director had understood the importance of having a system that would replace the thick binders representatives were using, eliminating the need to print thousands of pages each time there was a price change or a sale update, significantly reducing call times, and enabling the company to provide a higher service quality to customers. Everyone else thought they were about to get fired.

After a few hopeless attempts to assure employees layoffs were not planned any time soon, I stopped telling them what I planned to do and started showing them what I had in mind. I arranged a tour bus, selected twenty-five key employees from various departments, and took them on a field trip to the company I had worked for previously, where I was the content development manager of the first Knowledge Management system in Israel.

It was a pivotal trip, after which things had started to change quickly. Soon enough, they were urging me to finish the design of the system. I initiated a weekly meeting that included executives from every department, as well as representatives from the call center. In the meeting, I presented the system's progress and shared the new screens and features, which were based on surveys and hours of interviews about the call center's needs and wants. Those meetings had led to the establishment of a new organizational culture. One that was built on trust, mutual goals, collaboration, and understanding that success was the result of a true partnership. I had managed to make the employees from different departments feel responsible for and personally care about the system's success.

Every day, I went to work feeling a sense of accomplishment. I knew I had commenced an organizational change and had opened the door to a new era of knowledge sharing and future data mining. The implementation of the system throughout the organization was only the first step. For the last nine months, my team and I had been working hard to enforce data sharing, finding better ways of data sorting, fixing bugs in the system, and making lists of present and future demands.

My life was active. I was always busy. My schedule was full, and every little movement on the field needed to be carefully monitored, because it influenced other aspects of my life. In the few minutes I had to myself, usually while commuting to work, I thought my life was going according to my plan. I was married, a mom, and a career woman—the holy trinity of women in the twenty-first century. The three expressions were truly distinct, but the unity of them created the essence. I must confess I felt in control, much more than I felt blessed. It was a unique feeling of power, like living with a small but steady stream of adrenaline in my body, and it was addictive.

Yet now, I had a decision to make. I had to choose between leaving my career and living without my husband for two years. But there was another variant in the equation, and that was my son.

I had arrived at the playground and let my baby boy out of the stroller. I gently held up his soft little hands and helped him walk towards the slides set. We were the only people at the playground. Although it was overcast, a few rays of sunlight had sneaked through the clouds and made the sand sparkle. It was quiet, and I watched my son playing in the sandbox. Suddenly, he gazed up and murmured, "Dada."

I turned around and saw my husband walking towards us. "Did you hear him? He just called you Dada," I yelled with excitement.

My husband kneeled on the glittering sand, hugged our son, and nuzzled his neck.

"Yes, Dada. I'm your dad." My husband, who is rarely emotional, nodded, with tears in his eyes.

I watched them walk hand in hand out of the playground. I saw a man and a little boy who were sharing a newfound relationship. My husband was new to fatherhood, my son was new to the world, and together, they were discovering what it meant to be connected to each other. I took a deep breath of chilled wintry air and stepped behind them. I reckoned the fellowship was scheduled to start at the beginning of July. I had five months to think things through before making up my mind, but I had a crunching gut feeling that any decision I would make would utterly change my life.

3

LOITERING IS FOR RUNNERS–UP

From the time I knew my husband had accepted the fellowship, I felt restless. I sensed the winds of change following me wherever I went. Almost every day, I would wake up and my first thought was a question: what should I do? The nature of a question is to be answered, and when I failed to answer, more questions started to surface.

One question was why we were delaying the closing on a property we had looked at a while ago, when we visited our close friends in their new home in Binyamina, a town of 5,000 people in the Haifa District of Israel. Binyamina was founded in 1922 and named after Baron Edmond Benjamin James de Rothschild, who was a leading figure of the Zionist movement.

The Binyamina area is home to two of the largest wineries in Israel, and it is surrounded by vineyards and agricultural land. During the visit, we drove around and on the northeast side of Binyamina, we stumbled on a little paradise. It is called Moshav Aviel and is located in a pastoral valley, encircled by vineyards, groves, orchards, natural springs, and hiking and biking trails. The land was mostly dedicated to agriculture, but recently selected parcels were permitted a change of use from agricultural to residential and were offered for sale.

My husband and I fell in love with the small village that only had a population of 500 people. In the following months, we had gathered information about the area, the village, and the parcel's purchasing provisions. We considered it a great investment opportunity. The only drawback was the village's location in northern Israel, which made it far from both of our work places. However, my husband was due to complete his surgical residency within a year, and we couldn't anticipate whether he would stay at the hospital in Jerusalem or would search for a position elsewhere at the end of his training. My position at the telecommunication company was secure, yet I wasn't sure for how long I would want to hold it. Occasionally, specialized project managers like me choose to move on to a company that presents new challenges. We didn't know if we would build our home on that lot and live there in the future, but at the time, we had felt we wanted to.

Although we had all the information that we needed, we continued to delay the closing. As the months went by, I felt more eager to make up my mind about something, anything. I just needed to come up with a solution. Four months after we received the news about the fellowship, I became increasingly uncomfortable with our indeterminacy.

On a bright sunny morning in May, on my way to work, I felt it. We had to move forward. I recalled my university mantra, the one that I repeatedly chanted to my study group during our examination and marking periods, "Things have a tendency to fall into place." I had to believe that regardless of my decision about the fellowship, my husband and I would have a future together in a pastoral valley surrounded by fields and vineyards. I needed to feel confident that even if I chose to stay behind, our future together was guaranteed.

I called my husband. "Hey hon, we love the location of the village. We think it is a good investment, we hope that one day we will live there, so why are we holding back?" I asked bluntly.

"Let's go for it," he said.

I hung up the phone and turned on the radio. U2's *Stuck in a Moment You Can't Get Out Of* was playing. I grinned, raised an imaginary glass, and toasted "Cheers for getting out of a moment." It was 8 am and the news' theme tune was playing. Lately, every time I heard the tune, I would tense, waiting to hear the stream of information.

2001 was one of the darkest times in the history of Israel. It was the midst of the second Palestinian uprising (Intifada) that commenced in September 2000. Terror attacks, kidnappings, and suicide bombings became routine. In Israel, you could not escape the news. It was everywhere. Radio stations broadcast news at the beginning of every hour, and leading television networks followed when an unusual event took place.

Israel is a tiny place with about seven million people who are living in an area smaller than Lake Michigan, and the possibility of becoming a member of the "grief family" was quite high. Since the beginning of 2001, sixteen major suicide attacks and bombing incidents struck the country, leaving behind sorrow, mourning, and destruction.

Every breaking-news broadcast gave me an anxiety attack, followed by the same ritual. The questions: What happened? Where? Who was it? Where is my son, husband, family? Where are my friends? Who else do I know that could have been there? Who do I call first? The communication system—the cellular network—collapsed, and no calls could go through, I could only page my husband and call landlines. The information –I was glued to whatever media was available. The TV, radio, web, or any other data that could shed light on what was happening.

On many days, I had a heavy feeling in my heart and feared something bad was about to happen. We limited our lives to the boundaries of home and work. It felt unsafe outside. Most of our weekends were homeward bound.

On a sunny weekend in May, my parents and my three siblings came over for lunch. In my early twenties, I had enjoyed cooking very much. I frequently invited friends and family over for festive feasts. These were full-course meals that included different kinds of foods, with different textures, tastes, and colors. After I started my career and had my son, I didn't have much cooking time available, but now the situation in Israel forced me to stay at home more. I was happy to spend time in the kitchen. It felt like much-needed therapy, because it distracted me and alleviated the feeling of restlessness over the decision I needed to make.

I started cooking on Friday afternoon and continued on Saturday morning. The result was a delightful three-course meal that included Israeli cuisines that represented a melting pot of Middle Eastern dishes. We gathered at the small dining table, and my husband opened a bottle of Chardonnay from one of the many vineyards of northern Israel. We started our meal with deep fried red mullets that I served in a lightly spiced pickled lemon and sundried tomato sauce.

"So, how's work?" my father asked, dipping a piece of Challah in the brown sauce.

"Good," my husband and I answered simultaneously.

"I've been busy working with my development company on a new system module that can be set up to work with the document management system," I added, speaking very fast.

"I didn't understand a word you said," my brother interjected. "Actually, maybe only 'document,' which I know, because I need to fill out dozens of them after every shift, especially these days." My brother was an officer at the Israeli Police Special Patrol Unit that was dedicated to continuous security, riot and crowd control, and other special operations.

"I called you on Thursday, but you didn't answer," his twin brother, who was an officer at the Israeli Mounted Police Force, said. "I thought you were dead. We heard on the radio there was a huge operation in an Arab village east of Kfar Saba."

"I almost died. You can't believe what went on--"

"Boys, it's a nice Saturday afternoon. You don't really need to talk about that now," my mother said firmly, getting up from the table and collecting the empty appetizer dishes, while my father played with my son, who was sitting with us in his high chair, and my younger brother placed platters of fried eggplant with fresh herb vinaigrette dressing and a roasted cauliflower with Tahini sauce at the center of the table.

For the main course, I served lemony artichoke hearts filled with ground beef and Portobello mushrooms, and sides of basmati rice with toasted pine nuts and caramelized onions, and baked string green beans with Campari tomatoes, garlic, and oregano.

"You are the best cook ever," said my younger brother, and everyone nodded.

"What about New York? Have you made a decision?" my dad asked me.

"I've been so busy. I didn't have much time to think about it." At least part of that sentence was true.

"If I could, I would have left yesterday," my special operations brother said. "Don't you want to live in a normal place that is safe and you can go anywhere without being worried? A place where you can take your son to the playground without worrying. Somewhere with news about the weather and the opening of a new restaurant?"

"It's not like she doesn't have responsibilities here," my younger brother answered for me. "She worked very hard to build her career, and now she needs to leave everything just because her husband was offered a fellowship. No offense, bro, but my sister is talented, and she shouldn't give up everything she's accomplished."

"We're cool, I understand." My husband smiled. "She still has time to consider. My fellowship starts in July."

"Besides, who would help you buy a car, or pick up Ohad from daycare at the last minute when you're late from work?" my knight brother asked.

Israel is characterized by a close-knit culture which means you can always count on someone to come to the rescue. The week before, I was stuck in traffic, and I called my neighbor whom I hadn't seen for two months and asked her to pick up my son from daycare. She was more than happy to help. In such a culture, the people around you, family or not, didn't have to be your friends to care about you or help you.

"I'll be fine," I finally said. "I will not need a car in Manhattan, they have the subway, and I will find solutions, I guess. Maybe I'll take a break from work."

"You'll never take a break from work. You've worked since you were twelve," my brother insisted.

"What's for dessert?" my mom said, trying to divert us from the subject.

"I thought you'd never ask." I winked at her. "I made your favorite, Mom. A mascarpone cheese cake."

Everyone got up and cleared the table while my mother and I stood at the kitchen sink and washed the dishes. "Mom, what do you think I should do?" I asked.

"Anything you want."

"Yes, I know. But I'm asking you. Should I leave everything I've accomplished?"

"You are not leaving your accomplishments, those stay with you forever. You leave your career, your friends, your family, and your country. If you stay behind, you will leave your husband for a while. You need to decide what you can live with."

We finished washing the dishes, brewed mint tea, sliced the cheesecake, and joined the rest of the family, who were having a loud political discussion about the different ways to fight terrorism.

A couple of weeks went by, and my husband was getting ready to leave for his fellowship, and I was still considering my options. Indecisiveness isn't one of my intrinsic traits. Most of the time, I have an opinion or a clue about what to do in a given situation. Most of the times, fine—always, I have a backup Plan B or C ready to use in case Plan A doesn't work out. The fact that I was unable to reach a decision, and was putting it off to the last minute made me believe this decision was different from any other decision I had ever made. I had a feeling the consequences of my actions would influence my future in a way that I couldn't even imagine.

At the end of May, I had lunch during a work break with my manager. Dana was the Information Technology department director and had a phenomenal combination of non-confrontational yet non-compromising way of doing business. She almost always had a smile on her face, but she wasn't laid back by any means, and she usually got what she wanted. She knew I was considering my options relating to my husband's fellowship. I had told her that I had to choose whether to stay in Israel with my son and follow my career path, or leave for New York with my husband without knowing if I could find a job in my field. We waited for our courses to arrive, and I explained to her that I felt I was expected to freeze my life for two years.

"But you know what?" I asked, rubbing my napkin between my fingers, "Life wasn't meant to be frozen—well, that is until Cryonics proves otherwise, but it is safe to say that picking up from exactly where I left off is impossible. The reality is that two years from now everything will be different. You will replace me, and my team and colleagues will evolve and move on. Maybe some of my friends will move on too."

"Do you want to pick up where you left off?" she asked with curiosity.

"Yes, because I would leave behind so many things that I love. I am afraid these things will change during my absence, and I will be lost upon my return," I confessed.

"I understand, but no one can pause time. Things will change whether you leave or not." Dana observed reasonably while the waiter placed the plates on the table.

After lunch, we returned to work, and I wondered about the model of time. From the dawn of humanity, the concept of time has been a subject of study in science, philosophy, and religion, but it has always retained an element of mystery. However, my impression was that in this century, time had lost its mojo. We truly believe we have triumphed over time. We learned how to manage time, be ahead of time, kill time, have freed-up time, race against time, borrow time, and press time. The awakening from the illusion time is under our control could be agonizing, and frankly unnecessary, if we would only humbly respect time.

I had a choice. I could break up my family by having my husband travel for a two-year fellowship alone, or my son and I could join him, but this would come with an expensive price tag. I thought that the highest price I was about to pay was in terms of my career, which in many ways defined my identity. I was a wife and a mother, and most people would consider this sufficient, but I'd already tasted the forbidden fruit. I had a career, and I was good at it.

A few days later, on June 1, 2001, a Friday night, we were watching television when a breaking news banner appeared on the screen. A suicide bomber had exploded himself in Tel Aviv's coastline Dolphinarium dancing club. The next day, we learned the extent of the horror. Twenty-one Israeli teenagers, most of them high school students, and four adults were killed and 122 were injured. The following week was heartrending. I watched funeral after funeral of young lives pointlessly taken. Thousands of high school students escorted their friends to eternal rest, and families were left broken forever.

My husband and I were in the final steps of closing the purchase of the lot in the village. I was responsible for the paperwork needed for submission. During the sad week that followed the latest suicide bombing, I had juggled work, endless closing documents, bank and attorney meetings, and a doctor's appointment for my son who wasn't feeling well.

Finally, the week had come to an end. My husband returned home after a thirty-six-hour shift at the hospital; I hugged him for a long time, looked into his tired eyes, and whispered, "I'm in."

4

❧

CURTAIN DROP

*I*n June, I had announced to the company my departure come August. My team, of three young women, hadn't handled the news very well. We sat at the round table at my office and they asked, "How can you do this?"

I said my husband's fellowship was a unique opportunity, and I felt I needed to join him, especially since our son was so young. I explained the decision to leave wasn't only mine to make. If my son had been old enough to form and express his opinion, he probably would have wanted to stay close to his father. Yet, I knew deep inside my team's response was more than a simple inquiry. What they had really wanted to know was how an independent, competent, thriving career woman like me could walk away from everything she'd accomplished and follow her man.

Soon after I was hired as the project manager, I had met with Dr. S, the business consultant, who emphasized the greatest challenge ahead of me was leading an organizational change. I had realized I could design the greatest system in the history of Knowledge Management systems, but without employees who would voluntarily share their knowledge, the system would quickly be crowned as the most brilliantly impractical system in the company.

When it was time to hire my team, I gave a great deal of thought to the kind of people I would need by my side, who would be key players in the organizational transformation. I looked for candidates with a combination of specific attributes and skills. However, I figured while skills can be learned, personality cannot. Therefore, applicants were required to have a high level of emotional intelligence, be self-critical yet confident, and patient but vigilant. When I had first invited candidates in for an interview, I had not considered their gender. However, after a few interviews, I noticed women candidates matched my criteria better than men did.

At the beginning of the new millennium, the conversation about gender equality and feminism was less active than it was a decade later. But I had always believed in gender equality. During my two-year mandatory military service, I chose to serve as a tank instructor, one of the most challenging roles for women in the Israeli Ground Forces. Yet, I had also understood the recognition and acceptance of the differences between genders is completely unrelated to and should never be used to justify gender bias or impact gender equality. Each gender has its strengths and weaknesses and responds differently to opportunities and threats. Despite these differences, men and women should receive equal treatment, enjoy equal opportunities, and should not be discriminated against based on their gender.

I had not chosen my employees because they were women; I had chosen them because they demonstrated both the skills and the characteristics the job required.

My choice of employees had proved excellent. My team members had successfully balanced determination and aggression, empathy and rationality, and defused resistance with humor and flexibility. Together, we had accomplished change.

The young female workers considered me an example of everything a woman should be. But the same combination of traits I had sought in them, I had had in me. When it was time to choose a path for the future, those attributes influenced my decision to join my husband. At the time, I realized neither the cost nor the consequences of confusing my career with my identity.

I observed the young women in front of me, and I saw so much potential. I knew they would achieve anything they wanted. They had the skills, the willpower, and emotional balance every smart organization needs. "Hey, ladies, cheer up! You will be just fine, and I will be just fine too." I smiled at them and gazed at my certificate in business excellence that hung on the wall behind them.

After announcing my departure, I worked hard to leave behind a remarkable Knowledge Management system, a system that would make me proud some day when I looked back, many years from now. In record time, I implemented new features and screens that I had initially planned to introduce at a later point in time. I made a list of users' future demands and spent hours in meetings with one goal in mind—to leave a knowledge-sharing legacy. I wanted to make knowledge-sharing an innate organizational characteristic, one that future employees would naturally embrace.

At the beginning of July 2001, my husband left for his fellowship in multi-organ transplantation at Mount Sinai Hospital in New York City. I stayed behind to take care of unfinished business. Family and friends came to the rescue and helped me pack all of our belongings that I later had shipped and stored in an empty room at my parents-in-law's apartment. At the end of the month, our rented house in Kfar Sirkin was empty. I stood by the door and looked inside. I had so many wonderful memories from my time here. I remembered the incredible number of hours I had spent sitting in the kitchen designing the screens for my system during the late-night hours, listening to the owls' hoots and hisses. I smiled when I thought about the night my son was born.

I was thirty-seven weeks pregnant, and I had gained almost forty pounds that had brought with them all kinds of side and sound effects. The day my son was born, my husband was on call at the hospital, and I was alone at the house. I woke up at 1 am, touched the bed underneath me, and it felt wet. I called my husband and ceremoniously announced, "Great! Now I've lost control over my bladder."

"Could it be that your water broke?" asked the physician.

"Really, you think? I have three more weeks until my due date." I attempted to stay calm.

"I suggest you go to the hospital. I'll look for someone to cover my shift, and I'll join you as soon as I can," he said.

I wasn't prepared. I didn't have my hospital bag ready, my baby gear organized, but most importantly, I hadn't shaved my legs! I remember standing in the shower thinking, "I can do this. Many women go into labor and drive at 3 am to the hospital all by themselves."

At 7 am, my husband had finally arrived and found me giving instructions over the phone for last-minute quality assurance testing, just as the obstetrician announced I was seven centimeters dilated. Ohad was born a few hours later, and it was my twenty-ninth birthday. We had brought him to this home a couple of days later. It had been his first place of residence.

I gazed at the wall where the couch used to stand and remembered the first time I had nursed my son at home. Then I looked through the living room sliding doors at the orange grove, and I thought about the first orange I had picked off the tree for him and squeezed right into his opened month. In response, I had heard his first laugh. All those precious memories of valuable beginnings made me proud of what I had accomplished thus far. I looked at the three tall travel bags in front of me. In them was all I had for my new journey: some clothes for my son and me, toys, books, and a few toiletries. "Let my new life begin," I mouthed to myself and gently closed the door behind me.

5

⚬

NEW YORK, OLD LOVE

*I*t was an ordinary hot and humid August day in Manhattan when we arrived for the first time at our apartment, which was part of a complex reserved for hospital residents. The apartment was located on the sixth floor of a pre-war building on 96th Street between Madison and Park Avenues and had an unusual internal design. When I entered to the apartment, I saw a long hallway with rooms located only on the right-hand side. I walked down the long hallway and at the end, I found the living room, which was the only room with natural sunlight and a view to the street. The other three bedrooms faced the brown brick wall of the adjacent building. It was a big apartment by Manhattan's standards, and the fresh, strikingly bright white wall paint only made it look larger and emptier.

My husband had arrived in the city a month earlier just in time for his fellowship, and he had immediately dived into his work. He hadn't had time to set-up the apartment, but he had bought a few items from a couple who were preparing to leave the city. So when I walked through the rooms, I saw a mattress on the floor of our bedroom, a futon sofa in the living room, a dining room table, some plates, a pot, and silverware in the kitchen. The other two rooms had nothing in them but closets with sliding doors. On my first weekend, we rented a U-Haul van and drove to IKEA in Elizabeth, NJ, to buy only what we really needed. The fellowship's salary wasn't enough to cover our expenses in the city, and prior to our departure, we had taken out a loan and cashed in all of our modest savings.

After a week in the city, I found myself in a rather bare apartment, with a baby, no job, and no husband. He was always at work. Transplants are always unexpected, and he would leave the house before 7 am, go to work, and come back forty-eight hours later, during which he slept maybe seven hours that weren't even consecutive. I remember once when he left for seventy-two hours, during which time he flew to another state, harvested a liver, came back, prepared the organ for transplantation, and stayed for the operation, only to find out that he had to leave for another harvest. He traveled, came back with the organ, prepared the organ for the transplant, and took part in that operation. Although we lived a five-minute walk from the hospital, he didn't come home. The trouble of coming home to get an hour or two of sleep was too much effort.

I didn't recognize my life. I had little reason to wake up in the morning for anything. I didn't need to get dressed, prepare my son for daycare, or rush to work. I had an empty schedule, and sitting inside the bare apartment only emphasized the emptiness I felt. So I went outside. In the month of August, my eighteen-month-old son and I left the apartment every day at 8:30 am, and stayed outside for ten hours. We went everywhere. During the morning hours, I just pushed his stroller, choosing a different route each day. Later in the day, when the temperature warmed, we either stopped at a playground to enjoy the company of other children, entered Barnes and Noble to read books, or walked into a toy store to play. I would pack breakfast and lunch, and we stopped for meals in different parks and playgrounds. I learned the museums' free admission days, and we visited almost every museum in Manhattan. The city became my companion. As the days went by, I got to know it better. I knew what to expect. It was the place I escaped to from the emptiness I felt. It made me smile, kept me interested and engaged. It kept me sane.

In New York City, you never know what you will find when you leave your apartment. One day we found ourselves at a Lexington Avenue street fair, and the next day on the Annual Dominican Day Parade. A street performance or a public art exhibit is always happening somewhere in the city, and if you walk as I did, you will always bump into one. Those little surprises were my comfort; it felt as if the city prepared them especially for me, so I would not feel sad, lonely, and abandoned.

On the second weekend of August, my son and I visited Central Park. We entered the park at 5th Avenue and 76th Street, and we walked south towards the boathouse pond. We visited the beautifully crafted Alice in Wonderland bronze sculpture, and then continued a little farther and found the Hans Christian Andersen Statue. My son climbed up and sat on Andersen's lap, and I told him the tale about The Ugly Duckling, after which he kneeled and gave the small bronze duck a long hug. I sat on a bench while my son sat on the rim of the pond watching the model sailboats racing across the water. I looked around me and noticed that I was surrounded by families: parents and grandparents were all around me, playing with their children, talking with their spouses—laughing, hugging, and being together.

I came from a culture in which togetherness and mutualness can never be over-rated. It was the weekend, and when I lived in Israel, like most Israelis, my husband and I used to spend every weekend with our family, our friends, or both. As a matter of fact, not to spend our free time—no matter how rare it was—with family and friends would most likely have ended with an intervention. "We've noticed you have been distant recently. Is there something wrong? How come you don't want to spend time with your family? Are you upset? Are you sick? Should we stop by with a chicken soup? Is it the baby? Maybe it would be best if we come over. We should do lunch at your place on Saturday. Ah, and you should let your siblings know; after all, you don't want to insult them by not inviting them to join us."

Now I felt the absence of my family. My support system was oceans away, and I couldn't turn to them for advice, comfort, and support. My son came over and asked for an ice pop, and we headed to the nearest snack cart, walking away from the groups of people with their loved ones.

During my walks in Manhattan, I felt the desire to do something productive. These two years of fellowship could not go by with me at the apartment with a baby, without family and friends, and nothing else to do. I realized that for many women those two years would have been a dream come true. They could stay home with their baby, watch him grow, connect with him, be happy, and feel content.

I couldn't. I'd already had a successful career; I'd managed employees, and my decisions and recommendations had influenced the company's future. My life had been busy and hectic, but I had loved it. My day had started at 6 am and ended close to midnight, and I had only been able to spend a few hours with my son, but I had felt good. Most days, I had felt a sense of accomplishment, satisfaction, and pride.

As the days passed, I understood I could not be a stay-at-home mom. I didn't wish to be one. Some women can be stay-at-home moms, others cannot. I didn't think being a full-time mom was better or worse than being a full-time career woman. There are women who feel happy and content being housewives while other women feel happier working full time. I had chosen to have a career, and I realized regardless of which choices I made, I could never ever have it all. I don't think men or women can have it all. Besides, who wants to and is able to handle everything?

By imagining my life as a pie graph, where each sector represented the time and energy I spent, I found the sectors were not equal, nor would they ever be. Before I came to New York, the largest sector was my career, a smaller sector was my son, an even smaller sector was my husband, and a few itsy bitsy sectors were my family, my friends, and my hobbies. At times, my career sector was so large there was no room in the pie for my hobbies, or even my friends. I accepted it and tried to do the best I could to be good at each of the remaining sectors in my life.

It had only been a few weeks, and I already missed the person I once was. I liked my pie, I liked the distribution of the pieces, and I didn't want any other pie, as delicious as it may have been. I wanted my life back as it had been before. I wanted an uneven, uneasy, eventful, restless, fulfilling, and satisfying existence. I decided not to let two years of my life go by. I would look for a job, but first, I had to find a daycare for my son. I visited the hospital's daycare, which was located on our block, and it seemed like a good option.

For a week, I went with my son to his future daycare for a couple of hours each day. He seemed happy to meet and interact with other children. He was eighteen months old at the time and so were his new friends. They all had only a few words vocabulary so language wasn't an issue. The teachers were experienced in working with children who spoke other languages, because many of the hospital's residents, researchers, and physicians were foreign workers. They had communicated with the non-English speakers by using hand signals, face expressions, and picture cards.

The first week of September was the official beginning of the new school year, and parents were encouraged to spend time in the classroom with their children to ease the transition and reduce the separation anxiety. A few parents stayed longer than others and got to know each other. But one of them, Christine, immediately caught my attention. Besides being a successful director for two galleries, Christine was truly gorgeous. She had a slender figure, straight layered long blond hair with bangs, slightly slanted brown eyes, and a radiant olive color skin. She also had a charming smile, which she used a lot.

One time, when she was attending to her son who was playing on the carpet, she leaned forward, and I caught one of the fathers glancing at her thong. I went over and, pulling her aside, explained to her the situation. After we had left the daycare, Christine and I went to the corner Starbucks and started what was to become a lifelong friendship. I told Christine my story, and she said that she was familiar with how it felt to leave your country, friends, and your family behind.

When she was twelve, she had immigrated to America from Bulgaria, reuniting with her mother who had escaped Communist Bulgaria in the late 1960s when Christine was only two years old. She had stayed behind with her grandparents and was sent to America ten years later. I found her easy to talk to, partly because she knew how it felt to be a stranger in this country.

During this first week of September, Christine and I spent time together with the kids and without them. I loved her one-bedroom apartment on the second floor of a pre-war building on 89th Street and 5th Avenue, which she shared with her husband Todd and seventeen-month-old son Guy. The building was located a few steps from the Guggenheim Museum and Central Park. Although it was a small apartment, it was well lighted, thanks to the huge French windows that opened onto a charming patio with a garden.

On my first visit to Christine's apartment, we sat at the dining room table next to the window, had coffee, and talked about the way cultures interact with one another. I told her the day before I had met a woman who ran away from me at the playground after we had talked and I asked her for her phone number so that we could meet again.

Christine laughed out loud and said that she would have probably reacted the same way. "But you know," she said, "I find it easy to speak with people from different cultures. When I travel abroad and meet with artists and gallery directors, I find them easy to communicate with."

"This could be related to the fact you share a mutual interest and have the same objectives," I suggested, "But I think the differences between cultures are always beneath the surface, and those are the ones that steer the conversation or navigate the events. Bridging the gaps between cultures is the real challenge."

"I don't know if our differences are derived by our cultures or by the fact that we are simply different people," Christine challenged.

"OK, I'm going to need some papers and two pens," I said cryptically, smiling.

Christine came back with the items.

I divided the paper between us, gave each of us a pen, and used two picture frames from the nearby counter as a screen in the middle of the table. "Let's play a game I call... Identify the Culture. I will ask a question, and each of us should write the answer on the paper, then we'll show the answer," I explained the rules.

Christine laughed, straightened up in her chair and said, "Ask away."

"Complete the following sentence: Every good party should have..." We quietly wrote down our answers.

I wrote, "Food," and Christine wrote, "Alcohol."

"Love this game. I'm next," she declared. "Complete the sentence: The best way to spend a weekend is..."

I wrote, "visiting my parents, siblings, or friends"; Christine wrote, "chillin' at home."

Then it was my turn: "You talk with your neighbor about..."

"The weather," Christine wrote.

"Everything from purchasing a new car to your health situation to your relationship with your spouse," I wrote.

"I see what you mean, but how can you tell that these differences are the result of cultural differences as opposed to personality differences?" Christine quizzed.

"Elementary, my dear Watson." I grinned. "If you were to ask Israelis these questions, you can safely assume ninety-five percent of the time you will get the same answers. I believe the same holds true for New Yorkers."

Christine and I had many cultural differences, but years after we had left the United States, I always referred to Christine as my guardian angel.

She was there for me during one of the most troubled periods of my life; and when I was far from being content or happy, she accepted me the way I was, and always gave without expecting to receive. Christine was right to claim every culture consists primarily of individuals, who have the same need to be loved and valued regardless of their culture, and that basic desire is people's motivation to act the way they do.

"By the way, have you started looking for a job?" Christine asked.

A few days before, I had shared with her my feelings about staying at home without a job. "I plan to, but first, I need a work authorization. Yesterday, I applied for a social security number, and on the weekend, I'll gather my visa documents. I plan to go downtown next week to submit my papers."

A couple of hours later, I left Christine's apartment and walked around the corner to the Guggenheim Museum to visit architect Frank Gehry's projects exhibition before it closed.

6

❦

IN A CRISIS EVERY LITTLE THING MATTERS

On September 11, 2001, a beautiful Tuesday morning, I dropped off my son at daycare and was ready to take the 4 train to lower Manhattan to submit my work authorization papers. I was excited and grateful for this perfect Tuesday morning. Over the weekend, we had strolled downtown and passed by the World Trade Center. I had looked up and remembered the last time I had been on the top of the world. I was twenty-four when I visited New York City for the first time. I fell in love with the city and up there, on the south tower observatory deck, I vowed to come back. I planned on going up again that Tuesday, right after I had finished my business at the immigration office.

I was about to leave the daycare center with a few other parents when the administrator called out, "Something has happened at the World Trade Center." We looked at each other, and it was quiet for a few moments. Then mobile phones started ringing, and the front desk's phone rang as well.

One of the parents next to me answered her phone. "I see, OK, are you staying at the office? What? I cannot hear you. Hello? Hello? Honey, can you hear me?" she called. Then she turned to me and said that her husband had seen a plane crash into the north tower, but the call was disconnected before she could ask for more details.

The daycare office turned on the television, and the breaking news banner was across the screen with a live picture of the north tower's top floors surrounded by gray smoke and fire.

I thought about Christine. Her son was already in school, and I assumed she could be on the subway on her way to work downtown. I called her, but immediately got her voicemail.

A few minutes later, another parent answered his phone.

I heard a panicked voice on the other end screaming hysterically about a plane that had just hit the south tower. I didn't realize I was speaking out loud when I said, "It's on purpose. It's a terror attack." As a programmed robot, I went to my son's class, picked him up, and left the center as did a few other parents. The phone at the front desk didn't stop ringing all this while, nor as we were walking out the front door.

Outside on the street, people looked worried. I could hear the live broadcast from cars' radios and businesses' televisions. Many people were on their mobile phones, talking with spouses, children, and friends. Voices scrambled and I heard, "Leave work, go home, stay where you are, stay out of there, don't take the subway, grab a cab, I don't know, I can't say, what's going on? Are you close? Did you see anything?"

As I reached my building, a young woman approached me and said the Port Authority had just closed all the bridges and tunnels in the New York area and that she thought the subways would soon close too. She looked distraught, and I asked if she wanted to come up and call someone until we could find out more about what was happening. She said that she was on her way to her parents, her mom worked at building six; she couldn't reach her by phone and wanted to wait for her at home.

I went up to our apartment and turned on the television. Witnesses were being interviewed, and in the background were the two burning buildings. Two minutes later, my husband called, "Are you home? Is Ohad with you?"

"We're home, I am not going anywhere, and I'm watching TV," I said.

"This is too familiar; it looks planned, I think it's a terror attack." He echoed my thoughts. "The New York City Department of Health has activated an emergency response protocol, and I should stay at the hospital. I'm not sure when I'll be able to call again, we're waiting for wounded."

"I can't believe it. New York is supposed to be safe. America is supposed to be safe," I said.

We hung up, and I tried to reach my family in Israel, but the phone system had collapsed, and my call wouldn't go through. I knew the news had probably reached them, and I could only imagine how worried they must be. A day earlier, I had shared with them my plans to go up the south tower.

Another report came in about an explosion in the Pentagon. I looked at my watch. I couldn't believe everything had started less than an hour ago. What would come next?

I had tried to reach Christine, but her phone kept ringing, and then transferring to the voice mail. I hadn't left a message. This time, I called her husband.

"She's OK," Todd said. "She saw the second plane hit the tower from outside her office downtown. The subway system is shut down, so she's walking home."

I asked him to let me know as soon as she arrived home. "Do you know people who work at the World Trade Center? " I asked.

"I do know a few people who work in the area. I tried to call, but the phone system is a mess. My call couldn't go through." He sounded troubled.

"I hope you'll be able to reach your friends soon. I'm sorry," I said.

He asked "for what?"

"I'm sorry it happened to you, to New York, to America. I know the next days will be very hard, but try keeping to your routine and figuring out how you can help others," I answered, thinking about the terrible terror reality I had experienced before I came to New York.

After four hours, I managed to reach my family. I assured them we were fine. But nothing was really fine. I gazed out the window. The Upper East Side looked as usual, just a beautiful Tuesday in September with lots of sunshine, blue sky, and great weather. Lower Manhattan was a war zone.

Being an Israeli, I knew you could never be prepared for a terror attack, no matter how many of them you had suffered before. I was familiar with the extensive psychological and emotional impact of a terror attack, and I knew healing took a long time. I realized in the coming days the feelings of fear, anger, agony, grief, and guilt would haunt both individuals and the community.

A couple of hours later, Christine's husband called. Christine had arrived home after walking five hours from downtown to the Upper East Side. She didn't say much to him, just went to the bedroom, closed the blinds, and cried herself to sleep.

There was so much chaos on September 11th, and the media coverage was overwhelming. All around us, everything was loud and frantic, but two glowing torches illuminated the blackness with hope. One was the people of New York; the second was Mayor Rudy Giuliani.

All the stereotypes I had heard about New Yorkers prior to September 11th did not hold true after that day. Even as a foreigner, I felt the resilience, strength, and spirit that were everywhere. On Saturday morning, I went out for a walk with my son. We both needed some fresh air and a change of scenery after spending the last three days at home. The first thing I noticed was that the American flag was displayed on almost every building in the city. I saw candles and words of love and hope that were written on notes left by strangers next to each of the fire stations I passed by. At night, on the news I saw the rescue and recovery workers who were working around the clock at ground zero. They were sleep-deprived, covered with dust, but they looked determined.

On Sunday morning, I baked a few trays of cookies, placed them in small plastic bags, and drew a little red heart on each. In the evening, we took the bags of cookies and went to the West Side Drive just to cheer the workers who went in and out of the site. I had noticed many acts of kindness, and big and small gestures of humanity. Next to me stood a restaurant owner who talked with one of the rescue workers and gave him the location of his lower Manhattan restaurant. He had invited the workers to come and eat for free anytime they like. Other people around us held hand-written signs with words of encouragement and love. They offered the emergency workers bottles of water and food.

It seemed as though everyone was engaged in one way or another in the recovery efforts, almost as if someone had coordinated the events. But it was spontaneous, impulsive, and unplanned. It was a demonstration of unity and power that was simply astonishing.

While New Yorkers played the symphony of resilience and strength, Rudy Giuliani was the conductor who unified the performers, set the tempo, and listened to the sound of the ensemble. I first saw Mayor Giuliani when he appeared on television about an hour after the attack. He was on his way to the World Trade Center minutes before the south tower collapsed. Around him was complete chaos, but he was focused, candid, and direct. "People should remain calm; they should remain where they are, except if they are in southern Manhattan. If you are below Canal, you should walk out of southern Manhattan and go north," he instructed. Throughout the day of the attack, he was present and highly visible. We craved information, and he gave media interviews and shared what he knew and what he didn't know. I saw a man who looked troubled, concerned, attentive, and compassionate—all at the same time. He inspired unity and resilience, and exhibited persistence, devotion, and dedication to the cause, like no other leader has displayed since 9/11.

Mayor Giuliani's leadership through crisis struck a chord in me. I had always recognized the difference between the ability to lead and the will to lead. The latter is common while the first is rare. Over the years, I had observed leaders in business, politics, and Academia whose will to lead was so powerful they were able to convince people they had the ability to lead. Yet my cultural journey had triggered the observer in me and helped me focus on what people do, instead of what people say they do, ask the right questions, and use the information to better design my reality. This experience was a game changer in my personal time of crisis. Years later, when I needed to lead my family through hardship and pain, I was terribly distraught. Yet, I was determined, candid, and attentive to the needs of each of my family members. I inspired unity and resilience and helped us succeed.

7

⚘

THE ABILITY TO FIND MEANING

September 11th events were devastating to people all around the globe. The World Trade Center was by far the largest business center in the world. It was an example of what humanity could achieve by working together. I read that during the opening ceremonies of this building complex in April, 1973, the Chief Architect, Minuro Yamasaki, said, *"The World Trade Center is a living symbol of man's dedication to world peace... the World Trade Center should, because of its importance, become a representation of man's belief in humanity, his need for individual dignity, his belief in the cooperation of men, and through this cooperation, his ability to find greatness."* And so it did. The WTC tenants included about 430 companies from twenty-eight countries, having a wide variety of commercial activities. On September 11th, citizens of 115 nations were killed in attacks.

I can only describe the months following September 11th as a time of great sadness. In greater America, the shock was replaced by anger, but in New York City, I only felt the vast grief and immense sorrow. The cleanup began, and New Yorkers started picking up the pieces. People around me went back to work, dropped off their kids at school, attended funerals, and went home to their loved ones. Life had to go on, and slowly people did too.

Lower Manhattan was mostly closed, and many offices were damaged. I couldn't apply for my work authorization, and so I was at our apartment by myself. My husband was already three months into his fellowship, and he was always tired, stressed, and rarely home. My son was in daycare, and I had to pick him up late in the afternoon, so I had at least eight hours by myself. After three weeks of nonstop television watching, I felt sad and depressed. The personal stories, the analysis of events, and the pictures of the massive destruction made me reflect on my own personal narrative.

My time in New York was limited to two years. My visa terms dictated that any job I might find would be temporary. My work as a project manager required a long-term commitment, but before we had moved, I was optimistic and willing to compromise. I reasoned that a job would keep me in the market for the two years and, if lucky, I might expand my knowledge and acquire some new skills.

After three months in the city and after September 11th, I had no prospect of finding a job, and our financial situation became extremely tight. My husband's salary was only enough to cover rent and pay for daycare for our son. The other expenses were paid for with our savings and with the loan that we had taken out prior to our departure. We limited our budget to twelve-hundred dollars per month, which was almost impossible to live on in a city like New York.

At the beginning of October, the weather had turned. It was autumn in the city, and the leaves changed colors and started falling off the trees creating lengthy rugs of yellow, brown, and red on the sidewalks. One morning after I dropped off my son at school, I didn't want to go back to the apartment like I had done for the past four weeks. Instead, I walked to the Conservatory Garden.

I had first discovered the garden soon after our relocation, during one of the daily walks with my son. It was our neighborhood's garden as it was located a short walk from our apartment. It is a charmed place and you feel the magic as you pass through a stunning iron gate located on Fifth Avenue and 105th Street. The garden is composed of three small gardens, each with a different style—Italian, French, and English.

My favorite was the French garden where I used to stop, sit down on a bench, and watch the birds bathing in the water of the fantastic Three Dancing Maidens' fountain, a bronze sculpture that depicts three women holding hands in a circle and dancing in the water of the fountain. Their dresses are wet, and they have big smiles on their faces. Have you ever seen a rigid bronze sculpture that moves? I guarantee that if you sit by the fountain long enough, you will envision those ladies come to life, hear them laugh, and watch them dance. I sat down on the bench in the French garden and stared at the Dancing Maidens who represented the exact opposite of what I felt. I was lost and unhappy.

I started to question my recent actions: in the courtroom of my life, should I claim temporary insanity? Otherwise, how could I defend my decision to leave everything behind and join my husband for two years? What was I thinking? I considered myself a reasonable person. Before I had left Israel, my husband often turned to me for advice and so did my friends. At work, my colleagues backed up my decisions. They supported many ideas that seemed unorthodox or plain crazy, simply because they trusted my judgment. One time, they even agreed to prank the marketing department by making them believe we had accidently released a top-secret promotion, only to demonstrate the need for a system module they had passionately opposed. It worked.

After a couple of hours, I left the Conservatory Garden and headed back to my apartment. On the way, I wondered if it made any sense to leave a successful and promising career just to keep our family together. Anyway, my husband was hardly ever home, and when he finally was, the tension between us had started to show.

A fellowship in transplant surgery is highly demanding. The reality of transplantation surgery is its unpredictability. Bad things happened without notice and, when they did, transplant surgeons had to leave everything and go. My husband's fellowship was in multi-organ transplantation, which provided experience in adult and pediatric liver, kidney, pancreas, and small bowel transplantation. A liver transplantation is one of the longest and most complicated operations in surgery.

My husband was a fifth-year surgical resident when he started the fellow-ship. He was accustomed to long hours, chronic lack of sleep, and willingly paid the emotional and physical toll. However, he was not prepared for the intensity of the program and the exploitation of working hours he had to endure. The fact he was an International Fellow didn't help either. He needed to work twice as hard as the American Fellows to prove he was as worthy as they were. Years later, the ACGME instituted strict work-hour limitations that improved the conditions of fellows and residents.

By November 2001, I felt like a single parent. Literally, I had to deal with everything by myself. I had to drop off my son at school and pick him up every day. I played with him, read to him bedtime stories, and tucked him in by myself almost every night. I did grocery shopping and paid the bills. I was generally alone, and any problem that occurred, big or small, I had to figure out by myself. When one of my son's favorite toys fell through the window and the unpleasant building supervisor refused to open up the service door at the back side of the building, I needed to find a solution. And when we had $200 in our checking account and rent was due in two days, I needed to handle that as well.

When my husband did come home, he was stressed, sleep deprived, and emotionally drained. When my frustration was added to this equation, unbelievable turmoil resulted, which could only lead to terrible fights.

One weekend in November, my husband was finally off duty. I had waited for this weekend for three weeks. I had been yearning for some time with my husband, so that we could talk, and I would be able to share my feelings with him. I had that entire day planned out. We would stroll through the park to the Metropolitan Museum, visit The Quintet of Remembrance exhibition, the first major video installation to be acquired by the museum, take the elevators to the roof garden, and visit Joel Shapiro's metal sculptures display. The exhibition was about to close, and I wanted to see the cast-bronze figures that looked as if they came out of one of Keith Haring's drawings. Then we would go for dinner at Christine and Todd's apartment that was located up the street, and our boys, who had already formed a strong connection at daycare, would play together. I had longed for one ordinary family weekend like we used to have when we lived in Israel.

We were getting ready to leave the apartment when my husband's pager went off. A liver was on the way from another state, the transplant was scheduled to start in a few hours, and the fellow on-call was sick. When I realized my husband would not be able to spend the day with us, I was unable to hold back and I snapped.

"Why did you answer the pager? Are you the only surgeon available in this fricking hospital? They know it is your first weekend off in three weeks. You have a wife, a baby, a life. How can you do this to us?" I cried.

"I'm not doing anything to YOU. I must answer my pager; it was given to me for this reason. It's hard enough to be the foreign fellow that has to excel and prove himself without you making me feeling guilt," he yelled back at me. He left, slamming the door behind him.

After that fight, every act was an excuse for a dispute—if he didn't call when he had promised, if I had forgotten to do something he had asked me to, if he hadn't washed the dishes, if I wasn't home when I said I would. All these insignificant episodes that at any other time would have resolved themselves swiftly turned into out-of-proportion arguments.

I knew I had made the decision to leave my career and join him in New York, and I remembered thinking that keeping our family together was priceless, but, suddenly, I felt I had made a terrible mistake. I had an option to leave my husband in Manhattan, return to Israel with my son, and revive my career, but I doubted our marriage would survive the transition.

What had I been thinking? It was one thing to become an expatriate with an option to build our future in the new country. It was quite another story when we didn't even have the possibility of a future here. As J visa holders, we would have to go back to the country of last residence immediately after the program ended. The immigration system doesn't care how unique your program is, or how professionally attractive you have become. It doesn't care that American institutions or firms would love to have you, because they have a hard time finding someone like you. At the end of the program, you needed to leave. Roger, over and out.

J-1 visa requirements include institutional certification, which demonstrate you have the essential academic and employment background, and financial ability to support yourself during your stay. By definition, many of the people who meet those requirements have a spouse and/or dependents. What should the spouse do? Join the primary visa holder on their voyage to the land of the free, quit his/her career, uproot the children from their natural environment, or should they stay behind and break up the family?

America hasn't opened educational and professional exchange programs to internationals out of the kindness of its heart. America needs exchange programs to strengthen relations between the US and other countries. It is a win-win situation. On the one hand, the visitors gain training and experience in the US they can use to benefit their home countries. On the other hand, the US establishes its influence and power across the world. Furthermore, the visitors are not only receiving, they are also giving. They share their own knowledge and experience with the institutions where they work. During their stay, they may engage in research and development and could become part of a breakthrough innovation. They may contribute a fresh outlook on issues that might result in essential progress. At the end of their program, they may become so unique it is stupid of America to kick them back to the country of their last residence. America needs professional exchange visitors. Do skilled educated professionals need America? Is it worthwhile for professionals to pay such a high personal price to specialize in America?

In 2001, I paid the price. I left everything for two years and joined my husband. Today, I don't think my husband or I would have made the same choice. I know many talented, exceptional, highly-skilled professionals who chose to study in Europe, Asia, and Australia. In those places, they have an avenue to settle down without having to choose between education and family. They don't have to beg to stay; they are given incentives to stay. They are considered an asset, not a liability.

8

✿

A VOID

At the end of November 2001, I was unemployed, lonely, and alone in our apartment in Manhattan, post-September 11th. I returned to the routine I had adopted during my first month in the city. I would go out on the streets and wander for hours by myself, taking the subway, and getting off along the way, without knowing where I was, or where I was going. I spent hours in Central Park watching people walk past me. It was fall, usually my favorite season of the year, but when I sat on a bench and watched the trees shedding their leaves, I felt as if I was shedding my identity. It was the first time in my adult life I hadn't worked for such a long period. I didn't need to prove myself and be recognized for my success, but I had lost a substantial source of pride.

I was happy to be a mom and a wife. I thought that these were wonderful accomplishments, but at the end of the day, I wanted to come home to them as opposed to wait for them to come home to me. I needed outside assurance of my competencies, which were unrelated to my competencies as a mother or a wife. I needed this for balance. When I worked and had a crappy day where nothing went right, and I even sounded dumb to myself, I could always come home, and my son would look at me as if I was the best creation he'd ever seen. Other times, when I felt like I was the worst wife ever, because I didn't have any energy to listen to my husband's complaints about something at work, I could go to work the next day with a solution to a problem the team had worked on for weeks.

One night, I woke up from a dream covered in a cold sweat, dizzy, and my heart was racing. It took me ten minutes to calm down and feel better. I went to the kitchen and made myself a cup of herbal tea. I remembered my dream. I was a lioness roaming the African savanna with my pride that consisted of three lions, nine lionesses, and two cubs. It was twilight, and the Acacia trees looked like gigantic black mushrooms. The pride had just finished sharing a rhino we hunted a short time before. My mates were playing together, rubbing heads, licking each other, and purring. Suddenly I felt a pain in my lower extremities on the right side of my body. I looked down and saw that I had been badly injured by the rhino's horn. I licked my wound, and the group started walking away. I tried to get up, but I felt a sharp pain. I saw my sisters, the other lionesses, arguing with my cubs to follow them, and I tried to get up again. But I couldn't, and I had to stay behind, lying on the dry grass, watching my pride disappear into the dark. Then I woke up.

I sat at the dining table, holding the hot tea-cup. It was 3 am, and I heard a siren. It was an ambulance rushing to the nearby Mount Sinai Hospital. Apparently, I was not the only one who was hurting.

Nightmares were not the only symptom I had experienced lately. I also felt anxiety, nervousness, depression, irritability, and mood swings. I remembered a documentary I had seen about alcohol withdrawal. A few of the symptoms I felt were very similar to the psychological symptoms that might occur from suddenly having to stop drinking alcohol. Suddenly it hit me; I was going through a Career Withdrawal.

The fact that 'Careeraholism' is never included on the list of addictions doesn't mean it shouldn't be. I would argue that 'Careeraholism' is a remote cousin of 'Workaholism,' which justifies its being on the list. A workaholic is a person who prioritizes work over any other activity. Careeraholism is not about the action of compulsively engaging in a career and prioritizing it over everything else; rather it is related to the idea of having a career. Ergo, a 'Careeraholic' is a person who defines herself by her career. The effect on our brain of owning a career is so comprehensive and profound, that losing a career can promote withdrawal symptoms, which are similar to other addiction withdrawals.

Like many of my friends and colleagues, I used to define myself by my career. I realized that now, four months after I had lost my career, I was in a downward spiral. I felt unfulfilled, purposeless, and unimportant. It was as if I was not being heard. I felt I had been left behind while my peers had moved on. I was no longer responsible for my project, and I had lost influence and control. My employees were no longer mine; my office had been given to someone else who was now doing my job. I wiped a tear off my cheek, placed the empty tea cup in the sink, and went back to bed.

"What's going on?" my husband asked when he heard me crying next to him. He sat up and turned on the bedside lamp.

"I had another bad dream," I said, wiping my tears on my sleeve.

"Tell me," he asked.

"You should go back to sleep. You need to wake up in three hours."

"I'm fine, tell me," he repeated.

I told him my dream, adding, "I know that I'm being difficult and negative. I beat myself up for not being supportive. I'm angry with you. I feel that by accepting this fellowship you've ruined my career. I am not worthy anymore."

"Passive aggressive is another behavior you may want to add to the list," he smiled at me.

But I couldn't smile back.

Then he continued, "But, you are valuable. This fellowship is harder than any professional challenge I have ever faced. I need you by my side. You and Ohad are my family, and there are only a few things in life that provide comfort and support the way family does. Think that in the future if something was to go wrong with your career, it would be your turn to enjoy the comfort and support that a family has to offer."

"I joined you because I understood the value of a family. But having a career is equally meaningful," I answered.

"I haven't met a person who was loved by his or her career. Inversely, I have met people who loved their career in a way that destroyed every personal connection they had. You are worthy and irreplaceable to me more than you can imagine." He handed me a tissue.

"I am so sad. I may have made a mistake and ruined my life. Maybe there were more than two options? Maybe I shouldn't have chosen between my career and my family. There might have been a third option. I may have failed to find a way to keep my career and keep us together." I wasn't able to absorb either the significance or the kindness of his words. "Let's just go to sleep." I curled up on my side of the bed.

On the next day, my work authorization arrived in the mail. My already limited time in New York was getting even shorter, and the probability that I would find a job that was aligned with my expertise was close to none. I thought about the conversation I had had with my husband the night before. I knew accusing him for ruining my career by accepting the transplantation fellowship was inaccurate. He had been offered a great opportunity, and it was smart to accept the fellowship. In a world that has shifted into specialties, missing an opportunity to acquire a specialization, in a significant branch of surgery in a world-leading institution, would have been unwise. Besides, I had chosen to join him. I realized I had to find a new source of fulfilment and joy, and get out of the state of mind I was in. I understood my misery was very destructive, and if things didn't change fast, I would lose my marriage on top of my career.

Christmas arrived, and tourists came with it. The shops were busy again, and diners returned to the restaurants. The city dressed up for the holidays and made its best attempt to look cheerful and festive. The trees wore lights on their branches. Bergdorf Goodman's windows displayed virtues like hope, joy, mercy, and wisdom. The tree in Rockefeller Center stood tall and proud, and it was lighted with thousands of white, red, and blue bulbs. It was cold, but it didn't snow, and we went ice skating at the ice rink. It felt like a new beginning, and a revival was possible.

My husband had a few days off work; he left his pager at home, and we rented a car and traveled up north to New England. I suddenly remembered why I had made my decision to keep our family together and leave my career behind. I remembered how good it felt to be together as a family. I couldn't let our son miss his father. I couldn't let my husband miss our son. I wanted my husband to teach my son all the things I couldn't. I wanted them to share memories. My son was only an eighteen-month-old baby when we relocated, and I didn't want my husband to miss the 'first time' of so many things.

There are only a few things in life that deserve sacrifice, and family is one of them. At Norman Rockwell's museum, surrounded by families from different generations, I decided to keep mine. I would make the most out of my time in the city and upon our return to Israel, worry about my career.

9

⚜

LUNCH CLUB

During my empty days in the fall of 2001, I sometimes stopped by my son's daycare at lunch time. It felt good to visit him in the middle of the day and see his eyes light up when he saw me. I needed this comfort, and the feeling that I was significant and irreplaceable. I would sit next to him while he was pulling out the lunch that I'd packed for him earlier, and I would eat the sandwich that I'd brought with me. We sat in a group with other children and teachers, and everyone was busy having their lunch.

One day, a teacher approached me and said, "I have to tell you something, but please don't tell anyone. You make the best lunch I've ever seen. Your son eats everything; he is not a picky eater like many other children in my group. Every day, you send something different, and it is always healthy and looks delicious. I wish more parents were sending lunches like yours."

In 2001, America had the worst eating patterns in the western world. Eating patterns include not only *what* you eat, but also the *way* you eat. Americans ate too many processed foods, too much added sugar, too-large portions, way too many liquid calories, and they ate those alone, on the run, away from home, and without thinking about the nutritional value of their meals. An outside observer, as I was, could spot cultural phenomena that were not obvious to people who were part of the culture. After a few weeks in New York, I had noticed the local eating habits were far from being healthy.

My diet is Mediterranean, which is rich in fruits, vegetables, whole grains, legumes, and olive oil. I have been a vegetarian since the age of ten, but a Mediterranean diet is based on fish and poultry that are lean sources of protein, rather than on red meat, which contains more saturated fat. People who eat the Mediterranean diet use oils to cook, instead of butter or margarine. Salads are dressed with olive oil and lemon or vinegars. Snacks can be veggies, fruits, yogurt, or nuts. A variation of these items is also a preferred dessert. Soup is perceived as a fast solution for any meal. Chicken soup is also the go-to solution for many illnesses. Wine with the meal is highly recommended.

People who were born into such an eating culture mostly sit while eating; I truly dislike eating standing up. Eating in the car is considered a culinary faux pas, and so is eating alone. Thus we mainly eat in the company of others, and we always compare our meals. We believe eating habits can say a lot about a person.

My worldly culinary experience has sustained my eating preferences, and the Mediterranean cuisine is still my favorite. Moreover, I think there is no other place in the world that does Mediterranean or fusion Mediterranean cuisine better than Israel. After the establishment of the state of Israel, it became a safe haven for Jewish people who were scattered all around the world. Israel was a melting pot for varying cultures, and when cultures mix, food mixes with them. People from Morocco, Iraq, Iran, Libya, Egypt, Yemen, and Algeria brought their staples like Babaganoush, kebabs, couscous, shakshouka, matbucha, amba, and kubba. People from Greece and Turkey added burekas, tzatziki, moussaka, and Baklava, and people from Germany, Poland, Austria, and Russia contributed cholent, chicken soup, gefilte fish, schnitzel, chopped liver, knishes, kishka, kugel, strudel, and borscht. After sixty-seven years of blending, Israel has a superb fusion cuisine that is very much linked to the Mediterranean area where it is located.

I grew up with the culinary motto of "healthy body-healthy soul," and I value healthy eating habits. I believe what we eat is who we are, and when my son started to eat solid food, it was very important to me that he be exposed to a wide variety of foods and develop healthy eating habits. When I searched for a childcare center, I specified three key indicators of quality—the caregivers should be compassionate, the environment should be safe, and the food should be healthy.

Prior to our relocation to the United States, my son attended a daycare that served a daily breakfast and a hot lunch. I used to follow the menu to make sure he ate balanced and healthy meals that included fresh and cooked fruits and vegetables, grains, legumes, and proteins. The children were served only water or milk, and snacks included yogurt, oatmeal bars, fresh fruit, or chopped veggies. As a career woman, my time was limited, and when I was home with my son, I wanted to spend time with him, not be in the kitchen preparing food.

When we moved to New York, I was surprised to learn most of the daycare centers didn't serve meals, and parents had to send food from home. When I asked for the reason, I received answers such as "kids have different tastes," "most of the kids are picky eaters," "kids have many allergies," and the most common answer to everything-that-requires-rethinking was, "It's not safe."

I didn't understand how always-busy New Yorkers found the time to prepare healthy meals. Had I missed something? Was there a lunch fairy that I didn't know about? How come when I had a career and worked, I couldn't find the time to prepare healthy meals for my son, and everyone else did?

It turned out there was no secret, only a sad fact. Parents didn't make healthy and well-balanced meals for their children. Furthermore, many kids were not served nutritious meals at all. When the daycare teacher approached me at lunch time and complimented me about the lunches I made, it was because they looked very different than any other lunch in the room. I now had time and could cook meals that contained ingredients from the five main food groups, and they didn't include any processed food, added sugar, or liquid calories. They were also served in an esthetic way, and while it may sound physically impossible, we also eat with our eyes.

Healthy eating habits was a subject close to my heart and because of my interest, the answers I received from the teachers as to why a peanut-butter sandwich was the most common lunch weren't enough, and I went out to investigate. The playground on 96th Street and Fifth Avenue was the closest to our apartment and to the daycare center, and so it became my research field. I approached fellow parents who were playing with their children and carefully watched what they were putting in their mouths—it's a playground—who knew what they'd eat?

Most of the parents who visited the playground were working professionals. They didn't have time to cook food containing all five food groups, let alone worry about food presentation. They left for work at 7 am, dropped off their children at daycare, came back to pick them up at 5:30 pm, and wanted to spend some time with them outside on the playground. By the time they reached home, it was close to 7 pm. They had to give their children a bath, make something to eat, and get their children ready for bed.

One of the moms I knew from school had confessed, "You wouldn't believe how many times I fall asleep next to my daughter while reading her a bedtime story. Later, I wake up, take a shower, watch a little television, or do some extra work. I really don't think about lunch until the next morning, and I barely make it to school on time."

I assumed that in such a lifestyle, the five food groups are about as important to her as last winter's snow accumulation on the Himalayas.

All of the parents I spoke with cared deeply about their children's health, but many of them hadn't figured out how to eat healthy themselves, or how to feed their kids this way. On one occasion, I was sitting next to another father on the wooden beam of the sandbox while feeding my son with a spoon.

He turned to me and asked, "I'm curious. That smells delicious, but what is it?"

I answered that it was cauliflower, potatoes, and beet purée.

He looked down for a long moment before looking back up at me.

"You know, my wife and I might be contributing to our son's picky eater pattern by providing him with the food he is most likely to eat, because we cannot deal with introducing different kinds of food and experience rejection," he admitted soberly.

I had discovered many parents acknowledged the lifestyle they maintained prevented them from paying the necessary attention to their child's nutrition. When I asked, "If lunch was served at the daycare, would you choose it for your child?" some answered they would be happy to try it. Others said they didn't think their child would eat anything other than the food he or she was familiar with, and they would rather have their child eat something rather than nothing.

The idea of Lunch Club was conceived on the playground at the corner of 96th Street and Fifth Avenue. Lunch Club would be a food delivery service that would provide balanced, nutritious meals, incorporating all five food groups needed for healthy growing bodies. From the information gathered at the playground, I created a wish list compiled of everything that parents desired for their children's meals. The meals should be healthy, prepared daily from fresh, high-quality ingredients. The meal should look appetizing and appealing. Lunch should be delivered to the childcare center, ready to be warmed, and served in safe-sized bites. The flavors should be designed with children's palates in mind. The meal should be suitable as the child's main meal of the day. Finally, the cost should be affordable.

Although I loved cooking and was capable of making delicious and nutritious meals, it was one thing to cook lunch for one child and another to run a business that required, on top of cooking, a lot of administrative work. I introduced the idea to a friend of mine who had also joined her husband for a fellowship in New York. We both had children the same age who attended a daycare center and, like me, she had been exposed to the gloomy daycares' lunch reality. Besides being one of the most compassionate and loving people I knew, Mindy was also the founder and co-owner of a successful catering company in Israel that specialized in gourmet food for private parties. When her husband was selected for a fellowship in New York, she left the company and joined him for two years.

Mindy loved the idea of a Lunch Club and was ready to establish a partnership. On January 2002, we met at the County Clerk's office, located in the beautiful Supreme Court Building on Center Street in Manhattan, and registered our business.

The hard work was ahead of us. The concept of healthy eating habits and its contribution toward reducing obesity was novel. Everyone agreed eating healthy was important, but a majority of people did not know what healthy eating habits really were. Many Americans believed building IKEA furniture was easier than figuring out how to eat healthy. They ate some type of fast food every day and consumed much more packaged food than fresh food.

At the time, very few people thought American eating habits were a serious problem; consequently, very few attempts were made to change them. That is, if you don't count the transfer of the term 'fat' to the offensive words list, and its replacement with 'overweight.' Obesity entered the mainstream vocabulary only when it became clear a problem existed with American eating habits, and America was not only fat and overweight, but it was also very sick.

Mindy and I developed the Lunch Club's marketing materials and tried to introduce the concept to childcare center directors. However, the initial reaction was tepid at best. Some centers were not ready to deliver our brochure to the parents, or they wouldn't even allow us to stand at the entrance to the center and provide the leaflets to parents. Directors who were willing to listen agreed to host an hour-long session during which parents could learn about healthy child nutrition and sample our meals. Not many parents attended those sessions, but the ones who came asked questions, sampled the food, and some registered for the service.

After the first month of operation in a few childcare centers, it became clear children were not picky eaters. They ate almost everything that was served in their Lunch Club food container. Mindy and I cooked gourmet food for the kids, and they enjoyed dishes such as barbecued chicken with brown rice pilaf and caramelized julienne carrots with a side of red pepper and corn salad, homemade cod fish sticks with broccoli cupcakes with a side of Russian salad, and beef couscous with chickpeas and pumpkin with a side of red cabbage coleslaw dressed in olive oil and lemon. The food was prepared daily from fresh ingredients and from scratch with no added sugars or preservatives. It was esthetically served, and dessert was always healthy, yet fun. The kids enjoyed carrot muffins, zucchini mini-cakes, oatmeal raisin cookies, baked cinnamon apples, or fresh fruit.

During the first six months of operation, Lunch Club grew significantly and had members of all ages. Teachers and parents joined the program and purchased adult-size meals at the same cost as kids' meals. Lunch Club's value proposition was attractive, and the product didn't have any competition. There was no other company in New York City that offered delivery of healthy meals for children at daycare centers. However, in order to achieve profitability and growth, a financial investment was needed.

Mindy was already in her third trimester and planned to take maternity leave. We knew keeping the operation going would require us to either take out a business loan, or find investors. In the summer of 2002, both Mindy and I had less than a year left until our spouse J-2 visa expired. We were required to leave the United States immediately after the conclusion of our husband's fellowships and return to our last place of residence for two years before applying for any other visa or a non-immigrant status; we were undesirable candidates for a loan, and we didn't think investors would be willing to invest in a company with an expiration date.

August 2002 was Lunch Club's last month of operation. Our customers were genuinely disappointed; many parents wrote 'thank you' letters. They expressed the wonderful contribution Lunch Club made to their child's life. They mentioned how their child had learned to eat a wide variety of foods, and now could be taken to any restaurant in town. They expressed their appreciation for the design of the balanced and nutritious meals, but didn't forget to mention how appealing they looked. One mom wrote we had influenced her own eating habits, and that she had made many changes in her kitchen. The teachers and childcare center directors were also sad to see Lunch Club go out of business because it had provided an option which was very much needed for busy parents.

During the time Lunch Club operated and after it closed, I felt a huge sense of accomplishment. I had been able to make a small contribution and change both kids' and adults' outlooks on eating habits. Lunch Club's kids learned to love and appreciate healthy meals. Parents and educators were influenced by Lunch Club's philosophy, and many admitted they paid more attention to what they ate and the way they ate.

Eight years later, British Chef Jamie Oliver's Food Revolution show was aired on ABC. I watched Jamie's extensive efforts to convince school cafeteria employees to change their ways by replacing processed, unhealthy meals with tasty and nutritious real food for kids from aged four to eighteen. I smiled when I saw him explain to both children and cafeteria employees what nutritious food was, exactly as I had done eight years earlier. At the same time that Jamie's show aired, First Lady Michelle Obama initiated the "Let's Move" campaign to end childhood obesity in the United States. I wondered how many "Lunch Clubs" had developed in the United States during those eight years. How many innovative businesses from various industries with a potential for change were in the making when their originators needed to return to their home country?

10

⚜

OUTSMARTING FEMINISM

On a pleasant nearly cloudless September evening, Christine came over after work with her son. We often met after school at the park or at my apartment. The hallway was long enough for the boys to make their own private racetrack. They rode their tricycles up and down the hallway and used toys and blankets as obstacles along the way. Fortunately, the apartment below was vacant.

When Christine came over, she usually arrived with takeout food, wine, toys, or all of the above. That evening, we sat in the kitchen and opened a bottle of Veuve Clicquot. Christine appreciated good wine, and always said that it was one of the things that justified going to work for. She talked about her work at the galleries, and how difficult it was for her to balance her career and motherhood.

"Is it difficult because...you don't know how to balance?" I asked.

"Honey, if there is something I know how to do—it is to balance. I am the managing director of two galleries. Every day, I deal with artists and people from the domestic and international art scene. You cannot imagine the level of crazy I handle. If I didn't know how to balance, I wouldn't have survived a day. I balance better than the acrobatic troupe at the Big Apple Circus, I balance better than—"

"I get it." I laughed. "You know how to balance. So what is difficult?"

"I may have phrased it the wrong way. I know how to balance between motherhood and career. If I measure how successful I am in those areas, I would say that I'm doing pretty well. Guy is very well cared for. He is a happy little boy who expresses himself better than most kids of his age, and he is well-mannered. At work, I am doing extraordinary things. I am currently working with the Ferrari factory in Italy on the design of the UFO I told you about. Both work and motherhood get the attention they need. But there isn't a day that goes by without me feeling guilty."

"The Wizard of Oz, we want to watch the Wizard of Oz!" Ohad and Guy stormed into the kitchen. They had both discovered the movie a couple of weeks before and asked to watch it every time they got together. I played the tape, gave them a bowl of fruit, and sippy cups with cinnamon tea, and joined Christine in the kitchen.

She had already set the table with the take-out food she had bought from Republic, my favorite Asian restaurant on Union Square. I took a piece of grilled Japanese eggplant and reminded her, "You were talking about guilt."

"Yes, I was. Does it sound aberrant that I'm whining about guilt?" she asked.

"You know, over the years I have met extraordinary women. None of them was a superstar, a cultural icon, or a public opinion leader. These women came from different backgrounds, had different degrees, and different aspirations. Some of them had children, and some chose not to have children. They were all strong, determined, and capable women. In many ways, they were very different from each other, but they all had at least one thing in common. They all shared guilt, and that goes for me too, of course."

"What do mean you all shared guilt? What have you blamed yourselves for?" She nibbled on her watercress salad.

"Well, some women feel guilty for choosing not to have a career. Others blame themselves for choosing a family over their career or not having a family, regardless of their career. Many of my girlfriends felt guilty for not spending enough time with their children or spending too much time with their children. They felt guilty for not having enough energy left to take care of themselves, or they felt guilty for not doing enough to prove themselves. Many of my professional colleagues and I felt we were not making enough contribution to the global female effort that would eventually enable women to establish an all-encompassing equality." I took a sip of the French brut.

"That is so true. Things changed for me right after Guy was born. I feel guilty for things that I do and equally guilty for things I don't do. For example, I need to travel to Italy to supervise the production of the interactive sculpture. It is a very complex and ambitious project, and I will have to be away for a month at the very least. I delayed scheduling my flight five times, because I was unable to choose a return date. I feel guilty because I need to be in Italy, but even if I stay for the shortest period of time to mitigate my absence as much as possible, I will still feel guilty for leaving for such a long period."

I poured my curry vegetable noodle broth into a bowl, placed Christine's seared marinated salmon on a dinner plate, and took the chopsticks out of the brown bag. "A year ago, soon after I chose my family over my career, I felt the end of the world had arrived. My entire being was defined by my career, my ecosystem, and the society I lived in. This decision later contributed significantly to the guilt and worthlessness I felt for giving up my career, although it was the only way I could keep my family together. I needed a lot of soul searching to find my voice, to accept my decision, to feel self-worthy again."

"I know it was a very difficult time for you. In what way do you think society influenced your feelings?"

"In a way, I believe part of the reason I felt guilty and unworthy is because of the message women in power convey. A message that giving up a career is a troubling sign of ungratefulness and weakness, and that self-fulfillment and satisfaction have a positive correlation with climbing the corporate ladder and breaking the glass ceiling. After I chose my family, I felt I had betrayed my gender. However, the real problem of this peer pressure is that it can interfere with women's intuitive choices, and with women's abilities to succeed by following their innate characteristics. It took me a year to realize a woman's true right is to be who she is, follow her heart, and choose her own way. A woman should not have to feel guilty for her choices, when those are not aligned with the choices made by women who choose differently."

"I agree. Women do feel pressure to occupy executive positions. We are all aware that men outnumber women in leading positions in the industry, politics, and academia; they enjoy higher compensations, being promoted due to their potential more than due to their past accomplishments, and taking on only a small fraction of the responsibilities at home. However, I believe the way to change this discrepancy between men and women is by socially embracing the fundamental idea that women are indispensable and essential in every industry."

"Also, it would be wise to take the pressure off of women to score high-ranking positions, by either suggesting they turn into men and criticizing them if they don't, or making them feeling guilty if they don't measure up to those expectations."

Then I added, "Deciding to pursue a career is one of the most important decisions in life for both men and women. If you are in a relationship and have children, choosing to pursue a career is more significant than any of the other decisions you've already made. The decisions to be in a relationship or have your first child are completely within your jurisdiction, and at that point in time, those decisions impact your life the most. But, once you're in a relationship and have children, though your decisions are still yours, they are now within the family's jurisdiction as they influence your partner and children. When you have a family, every breath you take and every move you make has implications on your significant others' wellbeing."

I explained to Christine my notion about the difference between a career and a job. I said that each came with a different price tag. A career comes with a very hefty price tag, one of the most expensive prices one would probably ever be required to pay. While a job has rather defined boundaries, a career doesn't, and the individual is expected to give as much as she can. Career is a craft that requires a particular kind of skilled work, time, and energy, and its nature prevents it from being obtainable by all. Theoretically, everyone could pursue a career in one field or another, but practically it is impossible. A career can be very appealing to some people, while others will perceive it as a needless liability.

"I think women's capability to pursue a career is different than men's," I said. "Not because they are in any way inferior, but because of the compromises they are still required to make, and the price they have to pay. A hundred thousand years of evolution cannot be written off in sixty years. In most households, women are still responsible for many aspects of life, including their job. We can all roar that we are feminists if it makes us feel good. It would be stupid as women not to support women's rights, gender equality, and equal opportunities. But I agree a real change could be achieved by understanding women's potential contribution. If men are running the world, they'd better understand growth can only be achieved with diversity, and women can help them reconsider their traditional perspective —not by compelling other women to choose a career, but by supporting women's choices, and by helping women become successful."

"I do pay a high price for having a career and a family at the same time," Christine said. "The price goes far beyond the feeling of guilt I have to live with when I prioritize one over the other. I also don't take as good care of myself as I used to. I exercise much less, I am tired all the time, and I don't eat well. Most days, I feel that I'm out of breath. Maybe your choice was better than mine. You gave up your career, and now you care for your family. They need you, and you are there for them."

I watched the air bubbles in my glass rise to the surface and disappear. Had I given up?

When my husband's career got in the way of my career, I had two options—break up our family, or give up my career. Each alternative came with a price. Breaking up our family meant we might both be able to pursue our individual careers, but we would have lost our source of affection, strength, and pride, and we would have been haunted for years by our failure. High-achievers tend to dislike failure. Theoretically, my husband could have given up his fellowship, but it meant he would have had limited promotion opportunities in the future, which would have negatively influenced our family's financial prospect.

The second option involved giving up my career. Giving up my career could also have meant that I had failed, that I had backed down, that I didn't appreciate what generations of women before me had accomplished. It could have meant I wouldn't set a good example for my employees, and I was not the woman my friends and colleagues thought I was.

The truth was I had succeeded in solving a problem by utilizing a cognitive decision-making process based on my reality, not on my imagination, and I was more than grateful for the generation of women before me, because I made my own choices and designed my life according to my values and beliefs, not based on someone else's perspective. The choice I made suited my life situation, and if some women were compelled to judge me on whether or not I had a career, then I undoubtedly didn't need those kinds of friends and colleagues.

I traded my career for my family because I felt it was the right thing for us at the time of my decision. I became a wife and a mother for a reason, and I knew keeping my career would limit my ability to be the kind of wife and mother I wanted to be. I took a calculated risk and made a long-term investment. I traded my career for something matchless.

"You know, there is a big difference between trading one thing for another and giving up on something," I finally said. "I would have a very good reason to beat myself up if I had given up my career because my boss was an idiot, my employees were lazy, or my office didn't have a view. Giving up is not a good option for me under most circumstances. Trading, on the other hand, is."

"You traded, and I will probably keep on struggling with my choice to juggle it all. Am I wrong for trying?" Christine asked.

I looked into her eyes and smiled. "I don't think so. All I'm saying is that you should do what is best for you. I don't expect you or any other woman to make the same decision I made. I admire women who choose a different way of living, because I support a woman's right to choose, not because they choose to have a career, relationships, and children all at the same time. In their eyes, it is considered an achievement that is worth the price. I see it differently, and that is my right. The problem arises when those women criticize women like me for our choices, or when they try to make us follow in their footsteps. Their criticism can express itself in many creative ways, but the outcome is the same when "empowering women" becomes "overpowering women." Not only is it the polar opposite of feminism; it is the opposite of 'right.'

Many women know exactly what is needed to climb the ladder, but they choose not to climb it at all, or climb it on their own terms, or in their own time. Every woman faces different challenges, has a unique background and abilities to access education, and opportunities to open otherwise closed doors. Therefore, it is important women's choices be respected. Women who choose to climb the ladder at a different stage in their lives should be supported by the women who are already there. They should not be judged for their timing, their female characteristics, or for their choices."

"So, the trade you've made was a good deal?" she asked.

"Given the circumstances, I think it was." I smiled.

"Cheers for fair trade!" She raised her cup.

"L'Chaim," I answered, and we clinked our glasses. We cleaned up the table and joined our boys just in time to watch Dorothy clicking her ruby slippers three times and repeating, "There's no place like home."

The conversation I had with Christine on an ordinary September evening in 2002 was anything but ordinary. Years later, the discussion about gender equality received increasing attention, and while many women felt empowered to score high-ranking positions, even more women felt they collapsed under the pressure.

Over the years, I came to believe the idea that we can design our life to incorporate partnership, children and a career all at the same time falls short in the face of reality, mainly because we only have a certain amount of control over the course of our life. I cannot help but become irritated when I hear advice that suggests choosing the 'right' husband, having children at the 'right' time, and choosing the 'right' career path as a way to gain success. I had a career when I met my husband, and, when I had my first child, I had a path. I chose my husband because he was the man I fell in love with, not because I could have a career while married to him. I became pregnant because I wanted to become a mother, not because I had some time-off between the IPO and the company's next endeavor. Life is a plan subjected to change and partnership, and family can and should influence our decisions.

During the years, I never needed to be told to "lean in"; I have always stood up for what I believed in and went wherever I desired to go. I trusted my innate capabilities, skills, and experience to lead me to the positions of my choice; and I relied on my values, beliefs, instincts, and most importantly, common sense to guide me to make the right choice. Leaning in was totally unnecessary and could have seriously damaged my backbone.

If there was something I learned, it is the way to support women is to value who they are, respect their choices, help them excel in the positions of their choice regardless of their title, and encourage them to achieve their own goals, but not require them to achieve just any goals. Empowering women begins by respecting their individual choices.

Women who choose their own path will be more likely to succeed than women who feel pressured to turn into something they're not, or to pursue other women's dreams. According to the National Association of Women Business Owners (NAWBO), more than fifty percent of privately held firms are women-owned businesses. Those 9.1 million firms are beacons, and they celebrate women who stayed true to who they were and followed their own hearts.

11

THE HOURGLASS

After Lunch Club closed at the end of August 2002, I had only nine months left until the end of my husband's fellowship. It was almost fall in New York City, but unlike the fall of 2001, I felt joyful and optimistic.

The ways to cope with life's never-ending challenges are many. I believe the best ways include the principal of "never giving up." I cannot even count the number of crossroads I encountered since our relocation to Manhattan. Each crossroad had four options—quit, adapt, proceed, or accept. Most of the time, quitting seemed to be the easiest solution—why wouldn't it be? If I quit, I would not have to deal with the challenge any longer. However, even during sad times and in the midst of my great depression of 2001, I could still recognize quitting was a temporary remedy that would provide a short-lived relief, after which I would have to deal with a different struggle that was the consequence of my quitting. When quitting is not an option, the other selections become feasible.

I didn't give up. I stayed in New York with my husband and found a solution that fitted my reality. Many nights, after I had tucked my son to sleep, I sat by the window, looked up at Manhattan's starless skies, and whispered, "Give me the power to apprehend the reality I face, prioritize accordingly, and find peace with my selection."

A year after I traded my career for my family, I had accepted my priorities. I was significant and irreplaceable in the eyes of my family, as much as I thought I was for my organization. From the time I figured out that family was my best choice, I was determined to keep it together.

It wasn't easy to do, given the circumstances we faced. In the fall of 2002, a state investigation, initiated following the death of a healthy man who had donated part of his liver to his brother, had come to an end. The state had fined Mount Sinai Hospital for serious patient care violations, and suspended its live liver donor program. Since the beginning of the fellowship, the work hours and the demands from the physicians were well beyond reasonable or sensible. One of the investigation's findings was the healthy liver donor was admitted in a ward filled with thirty-four postoperative patients that were overseen by a single first-year resident.

From the time the state had started the investigation and by the time the findings were published, the transplant unit at Mount Sinai turned into a rink of accusations, allegations, and claims. The transplant fellows' conduct was scrutinized, and on top of their already highly-demanding schedule, they had to tolerate chaos at the unit. My husband became distraught and restless, and I silently listened to his complaints. Finally, only after the hospital was fined and the live liver donor program was suspended, did the chief of its liver transplant center agree to resign, and the hospital announced the entire program would be restructured.

After the chief's resignation and during the restructuring process, the second-year fellow, my husband's colleague, was unable to tolerate the extreme pressure and quit the fellowship, leaving my husband and another second-year fellow to handle the massive stream of transplants. Most of the time, my husband wasn't home, and when he finally was, he was physically and mentally unavailable, but we had both found ways to understand and support each other.

I had to raise our son mostly by myself, but when we did spend time together, we talked, walked the streets of New York, and enjoyed our family.

I don't think that up to that point I really understood what it meant to fight for what mattered to me. I'd heard the phrase throughout my life, but I didn't comprehend the meaning of the expression, and how much determination, devotion to the cause, and persistence one needed to fight for what mattered.

A year after the relocation, I learned to prioritize according to the benefit of the whole, instead of the part. I wasn't miserable, didn't consider myself a victim, or a martyr. I accepted that tradeoffs exist, and that life's musical chairs could benefit the entire family. I learned a tradeoff could be a very powerful tool for achieving whatever you wanted, but that it required patience and wisdom to trade only the things you considered replaceable for things that were not. In a strange way, not putting myself first felt appropriate at that stage in my life. It was important to me to become a wife and a mother; I considered it an accomplishment. However, I couldn't hang this accomplishment on the wall together with my degree, diplomas, and certificates for excellence in business. This accomplishment needed to be constantly protected, and, unlike other accomplishments, required maintenance.

After Lunch Club closed, I had to find another job to help support the family. We had already exhausted our financial resources, and we needed a second income. As much as I loved New York, love was an unacceptable method of payment at D'agostino.

At the beginning of November 2002, two things happened around the same time. I found out that I was pregnant, and I started to work for the education department at the Jewish Agency offices in midtown. The pregnancy wasn't planned, but we happily embraced it. The job was planned, but I cannot honestly say I had happily accepted it. It was an administrative position that didn't require any specific specialty. But I needed an income that would help us carry on until the end of the fellowship in June.

The nine months in Manhattan with a job, but without a career, felt as if they had happened to some else, and I was just a bystander. It felt strange to be involved in work that expressed itself as a business activity in exchange for pay, as opposed to the pursuit of lifetime goals, as I had done during my career. To do this job, I only needed training, whereas building a career required me to develop abilities beyond the training.

I would argue that career starts where the job ends. When you are first being hired, you really have neither career nor job. You've been hired, probably thanks to one or more of the following: your education, your experience, your recommendations, your personal-organizational fit, your person-job fit, and your ability to impress your interviewers. Once you were hired, you immediately tell all your friends and call your parents. You told everyone you had a new job, but really you were only hired. You have a job only after you've been trained and are able to independently contribute to your organization's bottom line. You can have a job for a few months, years, or a lifetime. However, you will only have a career once you have developed and utilized your very own core competencies, which allow you to deliver a unique value to your organization.

People prefer thinking they have a career because it sounds important, the compensation package is appealing, and the salary is higher—but what they really have is a job. They have good, interesting work that pays well, but it is a job, not a career. This is because careers require "core competencies," which are superior to education, training, experience, and charisma. Core competencies originate when you become an alchemist who gathers all his metals and transmutes them into gold, or in other words, when you use your education, experience, and training to develop abilities that cannot be easily imitated. Once you have developed and utilized your core competencies, you pursue your lifelong goals. As soon as you become valuable to the organization, you cannot be easily replaced, and your contribution is significant to the organization's growth—then you have a career.

Prior to our relocation, I couldn't imagine myself without a career. I believed that having a job, instead of a career, was like having a campfire without s'mores, television without a remote, or winter without snow –

otherwise, what's the point? At that time, I needed to pursue lifelong goals. I needed to develop a competitive advantage, and I needed to feel significant to the organization for which I worked. I love a good bargain, but in my professional life, I was willing to pay a much-higher price for a career instead of a job. After I had a career, I couldn't imagine I could ever go back to just having a job, but reality made me reconsider. I needed to support my family, and imagination alone was way out of budget. So I got a job, and tried to do it the best I could.

It was spring in the city. Central Park had turned green again, and the Japanese cherry tree blossoming was at its peak. I loved walking under the cherry trees and feeling the wind blowing the pinkish petals on my face. I was six months pregnant with my second child. Life was a sweet routine of going to work, spending time with my son, talking about the future with my husband, and getting together with friends.

12

A SEPARATION

*I*n June 2003, we were getting ready to leave New York, and I had to quit my job. After my last day at work, I went for a farewell stroll at my favorite place in the city, the Conservatory Garden. I passed through the beautiful Vanderbilt gate and went down the stairs. I took the left walkway of the Italian Garden, walked under the Crabapple trees canopy, and climbed up the steps to the Wisteria pergola. I was eight months pregnant and tired of the long walk. I sat on a bench, leaned against the gray brick wall, and watched the fountain's water gushing in front of me as if it were a geyser's eruption.

I closed my eyes and gently rubbed my belly in a circular motion. My baby pushed its feet against my hand, and I replied with a squeeze. I thought about my years in New York. So much had happened in my life. I had missed my family and friends during my stay in Manhattan. It had been the first time I had had to leave my support system. International calls were expensive, and so every weekend I called my parents, and alternated calls to friends.

During the first months after the relocation, it wasn't easy getting used to the highly individualistic style I experienced in New York. I mostly had to handle things by myself. I needed to find solutions without asking for help; at least at the beginning, I didn't know anyone that I could ask help from. I needed to explore my options and make decisions based only on my judgment.

The decision to open Lunch Club was solely mine. I had made this decision and pursued the idea without talking about it with any of my friends or family. If I had lived in Israel, I would have without a doubt talked about it with anyone who was willing to listen. But in New York, I learned to take risks and to bear the consequences of my decisions. And I needed to learn to do all that in a different culture with different norms and social cues.

Leaving my comfort zone, my country, my people, and moving to a different nation was challenging at best. The amount of data I needed to process soon after relocating was astonishing. A culture is a perfect example of Aristotle's observation, "the whole is greater than the sum of its parts," because a culture is much more than the norms, values, beliefs, meanings, notions of time, and cuisine shared by a group. It is exceptionally true in North America, which is populated largely by immigrants. The culture in the United States is influenced by many groups of people, and an immigrant or expatriate, if they wish to assimilate or even just fit in, has to process extensive pieces of hidden information such as subtexts, undertones, and nuances of the different groups who together make up the culture.

I got up from the bench and walked south towards the English Garden. I circled the small water lily pool, gazed at the Mary and Dickon sculptures, and thought about Frances Hodgson Burnett's words from the Secret Garden, "If you look the right way, you can see that the whole world is a garden." At that moment in the English garden after two years of living in a different country, I agreed.

I felt I had succeeded in my relocation, because I was able to fit in by putting the parts aside and focusing on the whole. From the first day in Manhattan, I was open to learn, adjust, and adapt. I stored my culture in a safe place, knowing that it would always be there when I needed it, and I opened up my mind and senses to a new culture. I closely monitored my new environment, watched and listened to the way people talked, walked, behaved, and responded to various situations.

On my first day in Manhattan, I had bought The New Yorker, and every day, I read local newspapers and watched local TV channels. In my early months in Manhattan, I spent most of my time outside on the streets, in parks, at museums, in stores, and I watched and learned so much. Adjusting to a new culture was one of the most *powerful* experiences in my life thus far.

As I left the English garden, I could swear I heard Dickon's flute play *A Bit of Earth* song on my way out. I headed north and walked towards my beloved location in the Conservatory Garden — the French garden.

If learning a new culture was one of the most *powerful* experiences, then one of the most *influential* experiences in my life was leaving my career behind and making peace with my choice to prioritize my family over my professional objectives.

During the first year of our relocation, I was passionately busy blaming my husband's career, or my husband to be more exact, for the demise of my career. During the second year, I accepted the fact that upon judgment day, I chose my family. I didn't give up my career but traded it for something matchless. Leaving my career behind opened a whole new world of opportunities. One of them was the opportunity to reconsider the definition of myself. I finally got it; I am more than my job title. I am who I am, regardless of my job title. I vowed that from here on, I would be defined by my actions, and my ability to make the right choices for me.

The opportunity to establish the Lunch Club and be part of a social change exceeded both my relocation's potential and personal expectations. It was a fine achievement to start my own business six months after relocating to a foreign country, but to start a business that changed people's outlook on life was amazing. The Lunch Club challenged the social consensus about food consumption and made an attempt to change eating patterns. If it had been allowed to develop, it could have initiated a food revolution.

I had arrived at my final destination. I entered the French garden, walked close to the dancing ladies fountain, kneeled down, and touched the water. I sat in the shade and took a deep breath. This place reminded me of how fragile we were. I had frequently visited the garden after September 11th when I was grief-stricken at the collective loss and my personal loss.

On one of my visits, I had met an elderly lady who had the same sad expression on her face as mine. We had started talking, and when she heard my accent, she asked about my origin. I told her about my husband's fellowship and shared with her the decision I had made. I told her that it was hard for me to find meaning these days.

She told me her family's emigration story from Berlin, Germany, to the United States in 1933. Soon after the National Socialist German Workers' Party took over in Germany, her parents were fortunate enough to obtain an American visa. They sold everything they had, bought transportation tickets, and arrived in New York when she was eight. Her father was a physician, and her mother was a teacher. She remembered how important it was for her parents to assimilate into American society. Soon after she started school, English became the only spoken language allowed at their house. During the early years in New York, her mom worked as a fabric presser in the garment district, while her father worked at a variety of jobs until he could obtain a position as a physician. Most of her family was lost during the holocaust; however, she had relatives in Switzerland and New Zealand. I asked if she lived close by the park, and she answered no, and that she was visiting her husband who was ill and had been admitted at Mount Sinai Hospital across the street. Before she went back to the hospital, she stared at the dancing ladies sculpture and said, "Meaning cannot be found, it should be created every hour of every day."

I sat by the fountain, thinking about the meaning I'd created during my two years in New York. I had followed my heart, conquered a few peaks, and adopted a new perspective on life. Not too shabby for two years. What was next?

We were about to move back to Israel. My husband had one more year of residency left, which needed to be completed at the hospital he'd worked at prior to our departure. Before we had left Israel, he had commuted an hour to work. As a surgical resident, his hours were long, and he had about ten weekday calls, and one or two weekend calls per month. Those shifts included emergency room coverage, which required him to stay up most of the shift. Back then, there was no supervision on residency hours, and residents literally lived at the hospital. I knew that we would have to tolerate those working conditions for an additional year.

I had no job to go back to, and we had a new baby on the way; therefore, it only made sense to live close to the hospital, which was located in Jerusalem. I'd never lived in Jerusalem. Most of my life I had lived in Tel-Aviv, and I didn't know what to expect. I reasoned that if I was able to successfully relocate to a different country, I should be able to live anywhere. It turned out that I was wrong, but on that late June, gorgeous sunny Tuesday at the French Garden, I was optimistic, excited, and filled with anticipation for the future.

During our last seven days in Manhattan, the goodbye parade continued. On the weekend, we took the 4 train to Battery Park, stopped by the Sphere that had been recovered from the wreckage of the World Trade Center, and took the Staten Island Ferry for a final up-close and personal look at lady liberty. The southern shoreline of Manhattan was my son's favorite trip in the city. In the course of the two years, we had spent time in the Battery Park area more than anywhere else in Manhattan. We had listened to afternoon concerts on the grass, strolled by the waterfront promenade, and visited the American Merchant Mariners' Memorial.

But my son's heart belonged to the World War II memorial that featured a bronze eagle statue. When he was two years old, he pointed at the eagle and enthusiastically called out "bird". A few visits earlier, he had walked towards the statue and then standing on his tippy toes, he had touched the base of the figure and, turning to me, said with a solemn tone that suggested the importance of what he was about to tell me, "Mommy, this is America's bald eagle."

During that week, we sold most of the contents of our apartment to a couple who had just arrived at the building. A few of our belongings were shipped back home. On our last day in the city, we went to our favorite playground on 96th Street and 5th Avenue to say goodbye to our friends. My friendship with people from another culture had opened a door to a whole new experience. It was the first time I'd had close friends outside my comfort zone—people who belonged to a different culture, spoke a different language, and had a different viewpoint. At the playground, I concluded having close friends from a different culture is probably one of the most interesting, inspiring, growing, educational, and joyful experiences in life.

13

ALL THINGS CHANGE

At midnight of July 1st 2003, we boarded El Al flight to Tel Aviv. I was thirty-six weeks pregnant, and the flight attendants were very concerned I would go into labor on the plane during the non-stop twelve-hour flight. After boarding was completed, we were transferred to the back of the plane, and I got an entire row of seats just for myself. My son had fallen asleep on my husband's lap, and I leaned back against the window and stretched my legs across the seats.

In twelve hours, I will be home. What could be difficult in repatriating? After all, I was going back to the place where I grew up. I knew the culture. I had my support system. My family and friends had missed me and looked forward to reuniting with me. I had left my old job, but I might have better credentials now, plus new experiences in working abroad and, thus, I believed naïvely that I could easily activate my professional network and find an amazing job. I conveniently forgot that before I had left for New York, I thought I would not be able to pick up from where I left off, and the following months proved I had been correct.

It was noon now, and a glimpse outside the airport's windows was enough for me to know I was home. Many people have that one sign that tells them they're back in their country. My indicator was the color of the skies. It was a hazy grayish blue that is especially distinctive to Tel Aviv. Our families were waiting for us at the airport.

"Is that all you have?" my dad asked when he looked at our four tall travel bags.

"Yes, and two years of unforgettable memories." I kissed him.

From the airport, we traveled to my parents' residence. We lived with them while we looked for an apartment close to the hospital where my husband worked. Two weeks later, we found an apartment in the old Malha neighborhood that is located in southwest Jerusalem. Before Israel's War of Independence, Malha used to be an Arab village. But on July 14, 1948 following a battle in the area, the Palestinians retreated and Malha was now under Jewish control. Over the years, Malha was modernized, and large housing developments were established on the nearby hill and on its eastern slopes, but a few streets remained as they were pre-war.

We rented the first floor of a two-story old house that was an architectural gem. It is a historic building that exhibits a profound influence of 19th century Ottoman architecture that included three feet-thick, sun-dried brick walls coated with limestone on the exterior, iron-framed arched windows, and soaring domed ceilings. When we signed the lease agreement, I considered the house a great source of inspiration for me. If the structure had tolerated Jerusalem over a century of vicissitudes, maybe I would be able to endure Jerusalem as well.

Three weeks after our return, I gave birth to my daughter, Gonny, and a couple of weeks later, we moved to our rented apartment in Jerusalem. My husband went back to work to complete his final year of surgical residency.

I had never lived in Jerusalem before, and I had rarely visited. Most of my life was spent in Tel Aviv. I first moved to Tel Aviv with my boyfriend when I was nineteen, and it became my home for the next ten years. I had completed my Bachelor of Arts degree at Tel Aviv University, and I had worked close to Tel Aviv where most of my friends were TelAvivians.

When we moved to Jerusalem, I had to go through the same experience as any other relocation. The fact both cities are located in the same country didn't relieve the adjustment process; on the contrary, it made it harder, because I expected to live my life in Jerusalem the way I had lived in Tel Aviv, but it wasn't the same, and I wasn't the same either. I had changed after two years of relocation in a different country and in a unique city. Manhattan is not like any other metropolis in America. The move from Manhattan to another city in America can be just as traumatic. Yet, the relocation to Jerusalem was surreal.

It was August, and Jerusalem was hot and dry. The neighborhood was small and densely populated. The streets were narrow, and our house was across the street from the synagogue. Every morning, I would wake up to one service or another. Next to the congregation's door was a small bench, and every time I passed by my window someone was there to bless me, my children, my home, my husband, and anything that they saw fit for the day, the time, or the time of day.

Most of the neighborhood's residents had known each other for many years, and were used to have window talks; while one was cooking in the kitchen and the other hanging the laundry out on the clothesline, or cleaning the windows, or knitting on the balcony. After a week, I already knew people's family trees and the black sheep of each family, what cleaning detergents were the finest, and the vegetable of the week at the Souk (marketplace) of Mahane Yehuda.

The tenants' dogs roamed freely through the area, and one had appointed himself our personal bodyguard. He sat by the gate, and every time someone went by, he stood erect and tall, hackles raised, eyes staring straight at his target, and started a long session of snarls and growls. The synagogue across the street was the most prominent landmark within the neighborhood, which caused the dog to lose his voice for a couple of days each week. Those two fairly tranquil days were the only time I could open the windows or sit in our small yard in front of the house.

I was living away from my friends and family, staying at home caring for a toddler and an infant, and rotating between unpacking and breastfeeding.

It was as though I lived in a bubble, completely disconnected from the outside world, but soon enough, reality kicked in.

It was the time of the second Palestinian uprising, which had started six months before we left for New York, and continued full steam during the two years we were away, and for about a year and half after our return. Three weeks following our move to Jerusalem, on August 19, 2003, a terror attack struck Shmuel HaNavi quarter in the city. A suicide bomber blew apart a crowded bus, killing twenty-four people and wounding over one hundred and thirty. Many of the victims were children, some of them infants.

My husband called and said his hospital had received many of the casualties from the bombing. He would not be available for the next twenty-four hours. I was thrown back to the last terror attack I'd experienced in New York on September 11th. I knew what to expect. There would be chaos, destruction, blood on the streets, and families who were desperately searching for their loved ones. There would be fear, grief, immense sorrow, and along the way, there would also be a response to the events, which would result in more tragedies to each side involved.

My husband came home the following day, looking troubled. He said he hadn't seen anything like it since the war, and he was talking from experience. He had been deployed in the first Lebanon War in 1982, when he was a young G.I. in the Israeli Defense Force.

The second Intifada's terror attacks in Jerusalem and throughout Israel became a horrific reality, during which the very basic condition of existence in any country— safety—could no longer be taken for granted.

We decided I would not use public transportation, and I would avoid crowded places. However, life must go on, and to make certain my children were safe, I had to find activities that sheltered us from danger. I started exploring Jerusalem and looked for summertime attractions. I discovered the Biblical Zoo was a short drive from our house, and it immediately became our favorite hangout place. The Science Museum had creative and interesting hands-on exhibits that my son loved. The Botanical Garden of the Hebrew University on Mount Scopus displayed a diverse collection of authentic Israeli species from around the country, and it became my favorite hideaway place. We visited the garden during special exhibitions or guided tours, or would just stop there for a picnic.

On a hot and dry September day around noon, I was shopping at a grocery store, pushing my two-month old baby girl in her stroller when a woman approached us.

"You're probably very busy, and you don't really have time to take care of yourself," she said.

I wasn't sure if she was talking to me, so I turned and looked behind me, but there was nobody else. "I had a baby two months ago. Umm, we recently moved to a new apartment. Er, I may have been busy, but not that…" I mumbled.

"Oy Gevalt (How terrible)! Do you realize that the way you've dressed disregards every rule that a proper, God-fearing Jewish woman should follow? Look at yourself. Your hair isn't covered. You wear pants, open sandals with no socks so anyone can see your toes, and a shirt without sleeves that's made of linen. Go home and wear modest clothes, and dress your baby properly too. Zol Got mir helfen (May God help me)!" She walked away, leaving me perplexedly staring at Gonny, who was watching us with her eyes wide open.

On my way home, I remember thinking Jerusalem was a very special place. It is one of the oldest cities in the world. The oldest part of the city was settled in 4000 BC, and it is sacred to three major religions—Judaism, Christianity, and Islam. Jerusalem has a unique combination of old and new, and on its streets marched the greatest rulers and religious leaders in the world's history such as King David, King Solomon, Jesus Christ, prophet Muhammad, Alexander the Great, Herod, and Suleiman the Magnificent. I admire Jerusalem's effortless power to touch the hearts of so many people from different nations and cultures. I don't know any other place that is capable of doing that the way Jerusalem does.

Tel Aviv is located only an hour's drive from Jerusalem, but the cultural, economic, and political distance between the two cities was in many ways similar to the distance between the Confederate and the Union states on the eve of the Civil War. While Jerusalem is at the center of a constant geopolitical conflict, Tel Aviv is doing its best to avoid any kind of conflict. While Jerusalem is observed and reserved, Tel Aviv is liberated and extroverted. This reality influences the culture in each of the cities, and people from one city have very different beliefs, values, norms, attitudes, and behaviors than people from the other city.

Jerusalem and I had very little in common. We simply were incompatible. Jerusalem was conservative at best, and I was more into experimental, unconventional, and irregular, much like Tel Aviv and New York—the cities I had lived in before. The chasm between Jerusalem and me could not have been more apparent than during my visit to the post office a week after my encounter with the lady at the grocery store. I was standing in line when I overheard two men talking behind me.

"This is Sodom and Gomorrah all over again, as it is said in Genesis verse 19:24 'Then the LORD rained down burning sulfur on Sodom and Gomorrah.' What is next?" asked the young man.

"When you let a bunch of faygala (homosexuals), running around half naked on the same streets where King David battled the Jebusites and where King Solomon constructed the Temple, you can expect pretty much anything," his friend said, referring to the annual pride parade that had been introduced in Jerusalem a year earlier, and had taken place for the second time two months before the time of this conversation.

"Soon they will open shops on Shabbat, sell pork at the market, and present shiqquwts (abominations) on the billboards. Oy, how did we get to this?" the first man asked.

"That's exactly right," an elderly woman, who was standing in front of me, said. "My Yankle would roll over in his grave if he knew. Love without Borders, they call it. Ah! It should be called No Borders," she protested loudly.

I stood between them, thinking about my last trip to Christopher Street in Manhattan, where love is celebrated out loud with no restrictions, criticism, or boundaries. I imagined that in Tel Aviv I would have stood in line at the post office and heard people talk about the new exhibit at the Tel-Aviv museum, a trip to the Far East, or Scorsese's latest *Gangs of New York*. But instead, I was living in Jerusalem, where my values were in constant friction with other peoples' values and norms. I thought, talked, and dressed differently than the people around me. Jerusalem is extraordinary, but like any other unique or exceptional place, it doesn't fit everyone, and it didn't fit me.

After I returned home from the post office, I thought about the idea behind peoples' demand for things to fit. We are satisfied when things fit, and not without a reason. Since my son was a six-month-old baby, I had presented him with developmental toys and games that challenged problem-solving skills. Each time he was able to fit the shape to the hole or the piece to the puzzle, he experienced satisfaction and was praised for his achievements. It can be called positive reinforcement or classical conditioning, but the outcome was that he, like any other child, learned problem solving is one of the outcomes of fitting things together. We all grew up with this basic notion, and after developing and mastering the art of problem solving by fitting things to one another, it is very hard to think about the opposite as a positive. Ironically, we need to experience, at least for a significant amount of time, friction and inconvenience if we want to grow and evolve, develop, and innovate.

There is a link between our society's pursuit of a comfortable, easy, painless existence and the desperate search for a fit. The idea that when things fit they become a whole is related to the immature notion people can have it all. If we could have been educated to think that uncomfortable, uneasy, and painful are as relevant as their opposites, we could have achieved so much more in life as individuals and as a society.

This is not to say people always should look for asymmetry, imperfections, complications, and discomfort. But when they do encounter such situations, they ought to view them as growth opportunities, instead of obstacles on their way to eternal bliss.

I sat at my son's room, where stimulating toys were scattered on the floor, and looked at his colorful abstract drawings, which decorated the wall behind his bed, and I remembered an encounter I once had with an artist at Christine's gallery. I loved visiting the contemporary art gallery that was located in the artistic and ethnically diverse Chelsea neighborhood, and talking with the artists and with the visitors who came in to view the collections. I often asked the artists about the connection between their personal life and their artwork.

Once, an artist told me he got his inspiration from New York where he had lived the majority of his life.

I asked why he had never tried living in a different place.

He replied that was where he felt most comfortable, where he could be himself and express himself.

I found his answer enigmatic, not because New York was not inspiring—it is one of the most extraordinary places I have happened to live in—but how can one be inspired and stimulated by the same things over and over again?

There is nothing wrong with a place in which you feel comfortable, or with a place that fits your personality. However, in order to grow, you need to go to different places, and often the most influential experiences may happen in places where you experience friction, feel uncomfortable, and where you don't fit in perfectly. You will probably end up leaving such places, but the insights you've gained will stay with you forever.

Jerusalem and I were not a good fit. However, the one year I lived in Jerusalem helped me grow in a way that neither New York nor Tel Aviv had.

Years later, I understood when I feel comfortable in a place, when things become easy for me, and I fit in, at the same time my curiosity declines, my excitement weakens, my interest deteriorates, and I lose a sense of urgency. Dissonance is what keeps people awake and alert, because the need to solve a conflict, which is embedded in our DNA, is the gateway for creativity and growth.

14

RESOLUTIONS

*I*n September, I began looking for an appropriate preschool education program for my son. The impact of relocation on young children should never be under-estimated as they are as sensitive as adults to moves.

When we relocated to New York, my son was a year and half and had an appropriate vocabulary for a child his age. He spoke about a dozen words clearly and linked two words together to form elementary sentences. However, soon after he joined the daycare center, he stopped speaking. I figured he must be very smart not to try speaking a language no one at school understood, but it didn't explain why he stopped speaking with me at home. I consulted with a language therapist who said he could be affected by the relocation and suggested a follow-up three months later.

It made sense. I wasn't the only one who had to deal with the dramatic change in the ecosystem; my son needed to do the same. In Israel, he had his routine, caregivers, friends, and stability. Suddenly, he was in a different place, where he didn't know anyone, and nobody spoke the language he understood. I knew he was going through an adjustment process, we both were.

After we had relocated to New York, he was the only thing in my life that remained exactly the same, so we became each other's anchor. For the first few months in the US, he was the most important presence in my life. He was the love of my life, my friend, my companion, the only soul I cared about. In a way, I, too, slipped into a silence, and our symbiotic relationship influenced us symmetrically.

As time passed in New York, my son started speaking again, only in English and with just a few words, not even close to the vocabulary held by kids his age. He was a happy child who got along with his classmates, and he was loved by his teachers, but his language skills were not as advanced as kids in his age group throughout our entire stay in New York.

Prior to our return to Israel, I did my best to prepare him for the relocation. We talked a lot about the change that could be expected in his life, and he was as ready as a three-and-a-half-year-old child could be. Once we had relocated to Jerusalem, I considered educational alternatives available for my son. He could go to a district or private Hebrew-speaking preschool, or he could go to an international school where he could maintain his language and culture, while gradually adjusting to the new ecosystem and to our new life in Israel. I chose the latter. It would be easier to adjust gradually; he'd already experienced a fair share of rapid change that most adults find hard to handle.

I enrolled my son in the Jerusalem American International School, which required a fifteen-minute commute from our neighborhood. It was a small school with only nine children in his class. Most of the kids were the children of internationals who lived and worked in Jerusalem. Some of the parents were diplomats, American Embassy personnel, news reporters, and expatriates working in Israel. The school had a comprehensive early childhood program, and the environment was nurturing, enriching, and safe.

Ohad loved his teachers, the other children, and the school, and so did I. In a way, the school's environment was the closest to what life had been like in Manhattan, and the farthest from the rest of my life in Jerusalem. The school's community was diverse, and the culture was based on values such as tolerance and acceptance of differences, and communication was respectful, polite, and non-confrontational.

On a Thursday afternoon, I took my children to the zoo. We visited my son's beloved Asian elephants, and the rhinos who were enjoyably sharing their spacious cage with the Screwhorn antelopes. After we had visited the petting corner, my son went to the playground, and I sat on a nearby bench, nursing my daughter when a young woman pushing a double stroller sat down on the vacant bench next to me. By her appearance, I could tell she was a religious woman. She wore a white silk head-scarf with a black border, a long-sleeved white blouse, a black skirt, tights, and lace-up shoes.

When my son approached me speaking in English, she asked if we were visiting Israel. I told her three months earlier we had returned to Israel after a two-year fellowship in New York.

"That's good," she said. "You should live in Israel. This is the Promised Land that was given by God to Abraham, Isaac, and Jacob. How many children do you have?"

"Two."

"I have five, all about one year a part, and I am trying for more, children are happiness. You should have more children," she recommended.

"How do you do it, caring for five children? That's a huge responsibility."

"Having children is the primary role of a Jewish woman alongside with being a wife and the household keeper. I am very happy to have five children, although I don't have time to clean and cook as I much as used to, especially because I work."

"Wow, how can you fit work in your schedule?" I asked, unable to conceal my surprise.

"I must work to support my family. My husband studies at the Yeshiva fifteen hours a day. I need to work to support us."

"It is probably hard to get by," I said.

"We are good. God is looking after us. We manage with my salary, a meagre stipend, and government benefits," she explained and asked, "Are you working?"

"Not yet. I'm a system analyst, and I work for high-tech companies. I would like to go back to work, but there are not so many high-tech positions in Jerusalem."

"You can do other things, I'm sure. Maybe get pregnant while you are looking for a job. You'll fulfil the greatest mitzvah in the Torah and keep yourself busy."

My son came back from the playground and asked to leave the zoo. I wished the young woman well and headed home.

A few days later, on cool and breezy Saturday morning in October, we were having tea in our front yard. Gonny was napping in her stroller, and Ohad was busy moving toys in and out of the tent my husband had set up for him, by his request. Ohad had recently become riveted with moving things from one place to another.

"You do realize I couldn't make Jerusalem my home, right?" I said to my husband.

"Yes, you've made it very clear, every day in the last three months. Where would you feel more comfortable?"

"I like the location of the lot we bought in Moshav Aviel. My friend, Ruthie, mentioned the development of the railroad enables an easy commute to cities nearby, and the area is really growing, especially among young families who appreciate the quality of life the village offers. I think we should hire an architect and start planning our home."

"What if after the residency, I have to work in the hospital's transplantation unit in Jerusalem? There are only three transplantation units in Israel: Jerusalem, Tel Aviv, and Petach-Tikva. If I work in Jerusalem, it will mean I'll have to commute for an hour and half every day."

"If we lived in Moshav Aviel, I would be able to work in many places. Living in or close to Jerusalem isn't much of an option for me." We were both silent for a long moment.

"I don't want to rent an apartment again," I said. "I think that it is time to settle down. I feel like a sand dune, when what I really want to feel is like a rock that stays in one place for a long time."

A few weeks later, we hired an architect and started to design our dream home in the village.

It had been four months after we returned to Israel, and everything seemed to work just fine; we were building our life together. My husband was finishing his surgical residency, and soon he would become an attending physician in a transplant unit. My son loved his school, where we had also met interesting people and were invited to parties and events at the American consulate and foreign news agencies. I was home with my daughter who was the most calm, happy, easygoing baby one could hope for, and I was busy designing our new home with the architect.

But then I received a phone call from Dana, my former manager at the telecommunication company I had worked for prior to my relocation. When I lived in New York, I had kept in touch with her mostly through emails, updating her regarding the events in my life. After we returned to Israel, she had visited me at the hospital after I gave birth to Gonny and mentioned a position that might become available. She wanted me to consider taking it when the time was right. Now she called and formally offered me the position. It was a dream job.

I was offered the project manager position for a new system that aimed to create a link between the Knowledge Management system I had designed and implemented, and the existing billing system. It was a natural fit for me, as I had explored such systems during the development of my Knowledge Management system, and I was interested in the design of this technology.

I was well familiar with the job description, and I knew what it meant to be a project manager, as I'd done it a couple of years previously. The design of my Knowledge Management system had started three months before I got pregnant with my son and continued while I was pregnant, which was a good thing, because most of the time I was so busy that I forgot I was pregnant. Three days after I returned home from giving birth to my son, I was having meetings with my team in my living room while breast-feeding. It didn't slow down until three months later when the system was fully implemented.

When Dana called with the job offer, I had just finished unpacking, with an understanding I would soon have to start packing yet again. I was home with a four-month-old baby girl, a son who was adjusting to a new culture and a new language, which was causing him some trouble. He needed a lot of support. At the same time, my husband worked close to a hundred hours a week, including in-house calls. On top of that, I was in charge of communicating with the local Construction Committee that required future homeowners like me to handle endless bureaucracy in order to justify its inflated budgets.

In my mind, I was ready to take the job and reignite my career. The storyline matched perfectly the scenario I had imagined before leaving for New York. I'd had a career, abandoned it, returned to Israel, and resumed it. Even better, now I had an option to reposition myself and resurrect my career. I was living in my very own Disneyland where dreams come true. Or did they? Was it feasible to add a career to my life mix?

A highly-demanding position such as I was offered required my full attention, long hours, sometimes weekends, and an hour commute in each direction. My son was already in preschool, and I could find a wonderful daycare for my baby. Then I could hire a professional nanny with a driver's license who would drop off my kids at school, pick them up in the afternoon, cook them dinner, wash their clothes, play with them, teach them new things, listen to their problems, comfort them when they felt sad, laugh with them when they were funny, read them a bedtime story, and tuck them into bed. It must be someone skilled, capable, and someone who they would shortly be calling Mommy. Was that in my dreams? Was it what I wanted?

It wasn't. I realized it was neither the time nor the place in my life to accept this job offer, and it was the second time I had to step away from first place, and trade my career for my family. Was I developing a pattern of prioritizing family over career?

No, instead I was choosing the wellbeing of three family members over one, which should be considered a good outcome of an educated decision-making process. Then why did I feel such disappointment, misfortune, and distress?

I thought about my friends and colleagues whom I had left behind when I relocated. They had all maintained their careers and families. I assumed that if it hadn't been for the relocation, I would be working and having a career just like them. I would have continued my work, had my second child, gone back to work, and accepted the promotion. What had disrupted the sequence? Could it be that the relocation had influenced my judgment? Or maybe it was the fact I had traded my career for my family once, and it was much easier to do it the second time around?

In retrospect, everything that had happened since I left Israel was the reason why I said no to that offer. I had changed. I was the same person, but my priorities were different than the ones I had before the relocation. My plans for the future were very different from the ones I once had. I had stepped out of the race, taken a break, and evaluated my move toward the finish line. I no longer defined myself by my job title, and I accepted the fact that in life, one cannot always position oneself first. Yes, because it is selfish to do so, and it is also a good recipe for how to end up lonely, even if you are not alone. The relocation created distance that allowed me to evaluate my way and forced me to think about many topics that until then were cerebral no-shows.

I missed the career woman in me, but I wasn't willing to prioritize her over my family's needs, not yet anyway. I had to help my son adjust, my baby girl to grow, my husband to finish his surgical residency, my new house to be built, and to prepare for another move. The third move in the past three years. At least this time, it was a domestic move, instead of a continental one.

Meanwhile, in the back of my brain was a yearning for something greater.

15

&

FACE-OFF

After a year in Jerusalem, we moved to Moshav Aviel, rented a small house, and started building our home. My husband finished his residency and stayed at the same hospital in Jerusalem to work as an attending physician at the transplant unit, after he had realized the other two options were unavailable. The transplant unit in Tel Aviv didn't have a position available, and the work conditions in the Petach-Tikva unit were disgraceful.

I enrolled my son in his first Hebrew-speaking preschool, my daughter in a small daycare program, and I became responsible for our home's construction project. Life was eventful and busy, but soon after, it became uncomfortable, uneasy, and painful.

Shortly after starting at his first Hebrew speaking preschool, Ohad experienced cultural and linguistic difficulties. The teacher called me and said he was sitting far from the other kids and covering his ears with his hands. When I asked him what was happening, he replied the class was too loud, the teacher spoke too fast, and the other children were impolite and took toys away from each other without asking for permission and never said "excuse me." *Welcome to a new culture.*

It is easy for parents to acknowledge the difficulties children experience when they relocate from their native country to the host country, because they are experiencing the same challenges. It is more challenging to recognize the difficulties children encounter upon their return to their primary culture. As an adult, the cultural norms, values, and attitudes were embedded in me, and I knew what to expect, how to respond to situations, and what was the preferred way to interact with different individuals from the society I was born in. For my son, it was a different story.

Bridging the cultural barriers required a lot of support, and for a period of time, I spent a few hours a day in the preschool, interpreting what he said to the other children, and helping him become more familiar with the social norms and cues. I have to admit I used this time in the class to teach some good etiquette, which we'd adopted in the host country, on the other children in the class with the complete consent, not to mention enthusiasm, of the teacher.

After six months in preschool, Ohad felt more confident among his peers and enjoyed going to school. However, the cultural difficulties concealed an unrelated linguistic problem that had always been there, but was harder to detect due to the move between cultures and languages. At the time we left New York, I knew my son could not express himself as well as other children his age, but the teachers and the language therapist attributed it to the relocation, and to the fact the spoken language at home was Hebrew.

After we returned to Israel, Ohad needed to use Hebrew as his primary language, and his teachers and I then explained the difficulties he experienced to the recent adaptation of Hebrew. Throughout his years in preschool and kindergarten, I knew he had some kind of difficulty in communicating. However, the experts we'd met with had suggested waiting until first grade to better evaluate his language skills and diagnose the problem.

The time that passes between the first recognition that something is wrong and the final approval can be very nerve-wracking. I considered all the language disability possibilities and ranked them from the most tolerable to the least. At the bottom of the list, as the least favorable disorder, I'd placed Dyslexia. According to the Mayo Clinic organization, Dyslexia is a learning disorder characterized by difficulty reading due to problems identifying speech sounds and learning how they relate to letters and words.

In 2005, Dyslexia had a bad reputation, and myths regarding the disability often harmed a child's self-esteem and confidence and influenced their peers', teachers', and parents' perception about them. I was troubled by the same falsehoods, and when we finally got the results of the evaluation in the middle of first grade, my fears were validated, and I found myself in an emotional turmoil. Questions raced through my mind—among them were: What kind of future would my son face if he was not able to read? Was there something wrong with his intelligence? Would he ever be a successful student?

What is real is that Dyslexia occurs at all levels of intelligence; students with Dyslexia can perform very well in school and can become leaders in their fields. Many people with Dyslexia are very bright and can be gifted in math and science. Children with Dyslexia learn to read, but slowly and with great effort. Students with Dyslexia work incredibly hard to achieve their educational goals.

My son joined the distinguished company of scientists such as Thomas Edison, Albert Einstein, Carol Greider, artists such as Ansel Adams, Pablo Picasso, Andy Warhol, musicians such as John Lennon and Cher, physicians such as Harvey Cushing and Fred Epstein, business leaders such as Richard Branson, Henry Ford, John T. Chambers, filmmakers such as Steven Spielberg and Walt Disney, entertainers such as Whoopi Goldberg, Jay Leno, and Keanu Reeves, and writers such as Agatha Christie, William Butler Yeats, and Philip Schultz. Not a bad group to be a part of!

Children with disabilities require an intense investment of time and energy and perpetual devotion. When Ohad was diagnosed with Dyslexia and word retrieval impediment, I read whatever I could get my hands on and expanded my knowledge of the field tremendously.

One thing was clear right from the start—my son would need continuous support from both his teachers and his parents throughout his school years.

At the time, dedicated Dyslexia programs were just being introduced in Israel, and many programs that claimed to offer programs for children with learning disabilities really focused on Special Education, which included communication disabilities, emotional and behavioral disorders, physical disabilities, and developmental disabilities. Dyslexia was different, and it needed to be handled with a distinctive set of tools.

The school in our district and other schools in the area didn't have any Dyslexia dedicated programs. I hired a private language therapist, who had used effective teaching strategies for kids with reading difficulties, to meet with my son in school a few times a week. However, it was hardly enough for building a strong foundation for success in school.

Dyslexia influences other skills such as memory, listening comprehension, and time management. Social skills can also be affected, as many children with Dyslexia feel inferior around their peers. I realized I should take an active role in my son's education, not merely as an advocate in school, but also in the daily practice of literacy skills.

My Bachelor of Art degree included language and literature specialties, and I had also attained a teaching certificate in language arts. I finished my undergrad at Tel Aviv University in my mid-twenties, without having a clue about what I'd like to do in life. I had an option to obtain a teaching certificate relatively fast, due to my B.A. credits. I figured a teaching certificate might come in handy, and since I was already a student, I might as well obtain it without too much effort. I was never a teacher; however, I had much appreciation and admiration for teachers as they command one of the greatest social responsibilities—shaping our next generations. Yet the knowledge I gained throughout my studies has served me more times in life than I can count. It inspired me to endorse values such as cooperation and collaboration, helped me to engage people with a cause, initiate new ideas, solve problems with creativity and imagination, and to do all that with compassion and a tolerance of failure. This knowledge became handy again when I applied it to help my son.

The attention and concentration levels of a six-year-old are usually short, but Ohad was committed to his success from day one. He wanted to master reading and writing and was highly dedicated to his studies. He would come home from school, eat lunch with me, and, after a short break, he was ready to work on his language skills.

We worked every day for an hour to an hour and a half, before I had to leave to pick up his sister from daycare. We read out loud, practiced writing letters and words, listened to audio books, and used computer games to master spelling and grammar. I always focused on his effort, not on the outcome, as I understood how frustrating it must be to do your absolute best and still not be able to succeed.

I invited friends from his class to work on homework together, and I explained to them my son's difficulties and demonstrated ways to help him. At the end of second grade, the entire class knew my son had Dyslexia, and he had a lot of help and support from both his classmates and his teachers. His self-worth and confidence were boosted, and he was a very likable, sweet young boy.

The biggest breakthrough came when I enrolled him in piano lessons. It started as an experiment. I knew that a letter was a graphic sign that represents a sound used in speech. I wondered if my son, in spite of the Dyslexia, would be able to learn notes, as notes are also graphic signs that represent sounds in music.

Life works in mysterious ways, and, if you don't try, you will never know what capabilities you may find within you or within others. Not only was my son able to read music, he loved the piano, and playing it became a special and intimate means of self-expression. His new skill became a constant source of pride and joy that has provided fulfillment to this day.

We found out my son had Dyslexia two and a half years after we had returned from our relocation, during which time we'd moved from New York to Jerusalem, and from Jerusalem to the village. Ohad was in first grade, my two-and-a-half-year-old Gonny was in a daycare, and I had finished the construction of our new home, and we had moved in. I had accomplished three very important goals—an adjustment to our primary culture, a new home, and good educational programs for my children. I was ready to go back to work, but I was still unable to jump-start my career.

We lived about ninety minutes' drive from Jerusalem, where my husband worked. An attending physician's schedule was better than a resident, but he still worked an average of eighty hours a week. He had at least one weekly call, and between one and two weekend calls a month—for which he was compelled to stay in-house, because we lived too far from the facility. The hospital benefited greatly from this arrangement as it gave them an in-house attending physician. Our household benefited a little less, because my husband's need to stay at the hospital came at the expense of family time.

The health care system in Israel is completely different from the one in the United States; however, it shares some similarities with the European health care model. It is a state-funded universal health care system, which is paid for mostly through income tax. Citizens in Israel must have a basic insurance coverage at one of the country's four HMOs, with eighty percent of the population belonging to the two largest systems. This model has its own deficiencies, which include higher-than-average private healthcare spending, extremely high hospital occupancy rates that increase the risk of discharging patients too early in order to admit newer patients, a higher-than-average number of physicians, and a less-than-average number of nurses.

During the last two decades, private medical services have seen significant development in Israel, as HMOs have built their own private hospitals—in small part to shorten waiting times for doctors' appointments and surgical procedures, and in larger part to increase their income. Over the years, increased numbers of physicians have started accepting patients in private clinics owned by the HMOs. It wasn't necessarily something physicians would have chosen to do, as they could only provide those services after normal business hours. However, low salaries urged many public healthcare physicians to seek additional sources of livelihood.

The hospital where my husband worked was a privately owned public hospital and as such, it was able to combine private services with public medical care. Through the private service, patients could select the physician who would be treating them; physicians who provided private services and procedures were able to substantially increase their salary.

This model was far from being ideal, as over the years something peculiar happened—the hospital started working for some of the physicians, instead of the other way around, as those physicians spent more time at the private clinics utilizing the hospital's resources, including healthcare personnel, laboratories, imaging equipment, and highly-advanced operating rooms at the expense of public care. Furthermore, most of the physicians that provided private services were seniors, while newer physicians, regardless of how talented and capable, were pushed aside and spent most of their time working at the public medical units.

After we returned from the fellowship in New York, my husband completed the last year of residency at one of the hospital's two branches, where he was highly valued for his surgical skills by his colleagues and the department chairman. However, this branch didn't have a transplant unit, and he was transferred to the second branch.

He was an enthusiastic, talented, exceptionally trained surgeon, but he faced the challenge of integrating into a different organizational culture that was characterized by weak leadership and passionate endorsement of individuality, instead of teamwork, by a poor evaluation process, and unequal compensation. He didn't receive recognition for his improved professional skills, and he rarely enjoyed the department's support for his initiatives, although the transplant unit included only two other surgeons, and his contribution was indispensable.

Throughout the five years he worked for the department of surgery, he was never provided an office by the chairman. Most of the administrative work that was part of his job, such as inviting patients for surgeries or follow-up meetings for patients, had to be done from the nurses' station, at his locker, or from the residents' lounge. While most of the physicians in the department enjoyed tenure, the chairman instituted a new torture technique—he offered my husband a one-year contract and waited until after the expiration date to renew it. At the end of each year, my husband didn't know whether he would have a job to go back to or not.

The situation at work impacted our family life for the worse. The life of a transplant surgeon is extreme enough without having to handle a malicious supervisor. A transplant surgeon never knows when he'll be called for duty.

In reality, almost every family's precious moments, special celebrations, or holidays were interrupted by a phone call from the transplant coordinator, after which we would not see my husband for at least twenty-four hours. My son, my husband, and I celebrate our birthdays in December. Ohad and I were born on the same day, my husband a week before, so it became a tradition to celebrate a triple birthday on the weekend between the two dates. Almost every year, that weekend was disrupted by work.

Additionally, our financial situation wasn't good. My husband was the sole provider, his salary was extremely modest, and he didn't have access to private care like the seniors at the surgical department. We were still paying off the loan we had incurred to fund the fellowship period in New York. Our expenses were high, partly due to the commute and related expenses as well as the Dyslexia therapy for my son, but mainly due to the extremely high cost of living in Israel.

I was responsible for the house and the children while patiently waiting for my turn. After we moved into our new home, and the children were happy in their education programs, I had to do the impossible and find a job within the realm of my skills and experience, but one that would allow me to tutor my son, and care for my family.

Almost three years had elapsed since we had returned from New York, and it looked as if the relocation was far behind me, but that wasn't the case. With regard or disregard to the difficulties each one of us faced, I missed our life in New York terribly. I cannot put it in words; when I try to articulate what I felt—a mixture of yearning, pain, and discomfort, like the same kind of feeling people have when they're missing a loved one—the description falls short. Almost every day, I felt misplaced and deprived. I felt as if I didn't belong in the place I was living in, but at the same time, I was light years away from where I wanted to live or could live.

There is a noteworthy difference between a disability and an inability. A disability is objective, inherent, cannot be reversed or changed, and people learn to live with it. My son has Dyslexia, and he will have to struggle with reading and writing throughout his life. The dictionary definition for inability is the state of being unable to do something due to a lack of sufficient power, resources, or capacity. I consider an inability to be subjective, because it is incidental, and it potentially can be reversed or changed. Thus, people should not learn to live with it. Often when I had to tackle a task, a project, or a mission that I'd never encountered, or the level of complexity was higher than I had ever handled before, my instinctive reaction was a withdrawal to the inability zone, or to translate –I had the feeling that I could not do it—it was impossible.

My husband's impediments at work could have been removed in one way or another, but at the time, neither of us thought of a solution. I started to realize my life was going in a different direction, and I thought I would be unable to change it. I thought I should accept it could take years until our two careers could reside under the same roof. I thought I should accept the fact my son would not be exposed to the best Dyslexia care, and probably would not be able to acquire a second language as it is unlikely for people with Dyslexia to achieve competency in a foreign language. I thought I should live where I was born, even if my heart beat miles and miles away.

Years later, I understood that most of the challenges I encountered in life and considered impossible to resolve were not only solvable, but could impact my mindset and turn into an inspiration for life. After more than my fair share of challenges, I can say there are only a few things in life that I consider unsolvable. There is always a way to handle challenges and come out stronger and smarter. The secret is not to be found in the manner of solving a crisis, but in the belief a crisis can be solved. When I force my mind to accept there is a solution, I have passed the most difficult stage of problem solving, which is to recognize there is an answer, and I am free to find it.

One by one, I solved the challenges that I once believed to be unsolvable. It took a lot of effort for me to live where my heart is, to make my son bilingual, and to enjoy the best practice of Dyslexia therapy. I learned how to be happy without being comfortable.

16

⚜

ALL YOU NEED IS OPTIONS

One of the reasons for one's inability to solve problems, lead a change process, or improve one's negotiating position is related to the concept of options. The first step in overcoming an inability is to persuade your mind that there is a solution. The next step is exploring the options available to address this challenge. However, options can be deceptive and illusory, because they really don't exist until we exercise them.

Options are all about the promise they suggest, and we hold the power or right to choose which options to exercise. Most importantly, we are responsible and accountable for the consequences related to our choices.

The concept of an option is related to a microeconomics theory that is called opportunity cost, which is explained as the value of the best alternative waived. For example, the opportunity cost of choosing my family in 2001 over my career was the income, promotion, and positive self-image I would have earned if I had kept my career. On the one hand, I lost fame, fortune, and confidence while choosing my family; on the other hand, I hoped to gain more in life, thanks to my decision to keep my family and to offset my lost career.

In my late twenties, after I got married, was hired as a project manager, and became a mom, I quickly learned every decision I made, or every option I chose, had an opportunity cost. Over the years, I had to forgo some really good options in the hope of enjoying something better in the future, and, in this context, the question about whether having options is good or bad was not philosophical, but practical.

During the first half of 2006, I felt life was navigating both my husband and me as if we were sailing boats with a broken mast, left to the mercy of the winds. At the time, neither of us felt satisfied or contented, but we both thought we were unable to change the situation.

On the last week of June, my best friend Ruthie suggested we go out for drinks and talk about what I was going through. Ruthie and I had known each other since we were twenty. We had studied at Tel Aviv University at same time. We had gone to the same parties, met the same people, and moved in with our boyfriends, and later moved out. Ruthie was with me when I first met a compassionate young surgical resident who later became my husband. I introduced her to my roommate, who later became her husband. We got married and had children all around the same time. Over the years, we became each other's compass. Each time one of us had lost her way, the other would come to the rescue. The best thing about having this kind of friendship is the intimate knowledge we share about each other. We could discern by the sound of each other's voice or by a single comment that something was wrong.

We went to a quiet bistro close to home. We ordered a bottle of Merlot from the local Tishbi winery. I often rode my bike close to the company's vineyards on the slopes near my home, and watching the way they cared for the grapes, I had figured their wine would probably have a great soul.

"What's going on?" Ruthie diverted me from the mulberry fields back to the bistro's chestnut-colored tables.

I inhaled deeply. "I know I should be thankful for the many things we've been able to accomplish. I don't take anything for granted. But we are not in a good place. When I wake up in the morning, I feel like I'm in a survival mode. I hardly see my husband. I feel his work is so all consuming there's no room left for us. He stays at the hospital at least two nights a week, and one or two weekends a month. When he stays at the hospital, he crashes on the sofa in his colleague's office or in the physicians' lounge. I almost think the transplantation fellowship was a mistake, given the intensity of the work and the extremely modest compensation," I complained and took a sip of the wine that displayed a hint of blackcurrant and strawberry.

"Does he like his job?" She nibbled on a piece of a local dairy semi-soft goat cheese from the cheese platter.

"He likes his work. He is an incredible diagnostician and a very talented surgeon. But his chairman is a nightmare. It almost seems like he does everything he possibly can to make my husband's life miserable."

"Still no office?"

"No office, no access to private practice, no respect, not enough money, and most importantly, no options." I summarized the reality.

Ruthie was a Human Resource manager in a high-tech company. Every time she needed to find a solution to a problem, she would rationally and professionally analyze the situation.

"Here's the thing," she finally said after swallowing a piece of the freshly baked country loaf. "When it comes to problem solving, people exhibit three different approaches to options. People who believe in their inability to solve problems may really be fearful of the cost related to the solution of their choice. This fear is paralyzing and leads to a complete standstill, where the problem exists and the solution is available, but nothing is done to solve it. Those people will convince themselves there are no solutions available. For them, having options is neither good nor bad.

"Other people will recognize the problem, believe in their ability to solve it, find different solutions, but cannot choose between the options because, again, each option has an opportunity cost that they know they will have to be responsible or accountable for. Their indecision results in the same gridlock. For those people, having options is bad.

"Lastly, there are people who solve problems by collecting as many options as they can find. To them, having options is the most magnificent thing. These people are aware of the opportunity cost, but they also know that in order to reduce risk, they have to diversify the portfolio," she concluded.

"What you are really saying is that in life, I should always have options, and I should never think a problem has only one solution. It could very well be that the best solutions are the ones created by melding a few options into one," I argued.

"The reason for which the problem-solving process is complex is related to the need to overcome several inner barriers. First, you need to ignore your instinct to avoid the unfamiliar threat and then find a way to believe a solution can be found. Second, you need to use every ounce of imagination and creativity to increase the number of options you could use to solve the problem. Third, you need to narrow down by omitting or combining options, and only keep the option that is most likely to succeed. Finally, you need to take a leap of faith and introduce the solution to the problem, while considering the fact it may not be a match made in heaven, and you will have to apply your second-best option." She smiled and took a sip of wine.

"Well, there is no wonder people feel unable to solve problems as they require mental resources that are not always within reach." I chuckled.

"But a good way to take the fear of failure out of the equation is to think of as many options as you can to solve a problem without excluding any option, no matter how irrational and unrealistic it may be. When my friend was single and desperately wanted to find the love of her life and get married, I suggested she look for a husband while she had a boyfriend. When she looked for her dream job, I suggested she find any job in her field, and from there search for her dream job. I was aware it sounded crazy, but she did have a boyfriend when she met her husband; and she scored a high-ranking position in a leading company while she was holding a position that was two sizes smaller. The trick is to manipulate your mind into thinking that you have already chosen, and then you're free to explore more options. The more options you have, the greater the possibility of finding a solution, and solving a problem," Ruthie declared.

It was getting late, and the delicious Merlot was empty. We parted, and on my way home, I deliberated over our conversation. In my everyday life, I am busy, preoccupied, and restless, so often I act by inaction and don't solve a thing. Other times, I perpetually weigh and rank options by importance and impact, until I lose the momentum and leave the problem hanging. I remember thinking I needed to do better than that. I needed to always have options and take risks. My ability to develop risk tolerance, and perceive failure as growing pains, could open doors for me that may have been closed for a very long time.

People are far more capable than they think, but they don't dare take chances because the cost might be too high, or the risk too dangerous. If anything, history has taught us humanity pushes boundaries all the time. Technology that was once considered fiction has become reality; rivalries that lasted decades have come to an understanding; infectious diseases that killed millions have become extinct or an effective cure was invented. We are everything but incapable. Even if I take an educated risk and fail, nothing irredeemable will happen. However, a risk should be taken even when other options are available, no matter how good or bad they may be.

At the time, I was unsatisfied on many fronts of my life; I didn't have a sense of fulfillment, I didn't feel as if I belonged, I didn't like my life. I knew I had a problem, and I believed there was a solution, but I couldn't collect options.

The fact I was a part of a family made things even more complicated, because some problems were not even mine, but they were entangled, or had an influence on my problems. My husband's career was highly demanding and couldn't coexist with a second career in the same house. The fact that I wanted a career but couldn't pursue one was a big problem. Plus, my husband was unhappy at the hospital, and it influenced our family's wellbeing. My son was not getting proper Dyslexia treatment, which kept me awake at night, thinking about the future he might face. Our financial situation was not good, and we needed the help of our parents, which made me feel powerless. I didn't feel as if I belonged in the place where I lived, but I couldn't leave, because there wasn't only me to consider, but my husband, and my family as well.

A thick fog surrounded my brain each time I tried to find options. I knew I could not solve problems without having options, but I did do two things. One, I registered for the annual United States Diversity Immigrant Visa Program known as the green card lottery, and two, I started looking for a job.

17

❧

A CONFLICT OF INTERESTS

On July 12, 2006, more than two years after the end of the second Palestinian uprising that took the lives of hundreds of Israelis and destroyed thousands of families, and a year after the unilateral withdrawal of Israel from the Gaza Strip that resulted in a domestic conflict that fell short from becoming a civil war as Israel needed to remove thousands of Israeli citizens from their homes, the second Lebanon War started.

Israelis are accustomed to breaking news broadcasts. I think that after sixty-seven years of terror attacks with a few war breaks, the Israeli media should invent a new phrase to distinguish between ordinary breaking news, like the news that sovereign nations use to describe an event currently occurring or developing, and news about a terror attack or war. Something along the lines of 'war newscast,' 'terror attack special report,' 'never-ending conflict update,' or 'enough is enough newsflash,' would work well.

On Wednesday, July 12th, a news broadcast announced that the Hezbollah, a terrorist organization based in southern Lebanon, had fired rockets on several Israeli northern towns. Troops crossed the border from Lebanon into Israel, ambushed two Israeli military patrol vehicles, killing three soldiers and abducting two other soldiers.

It was quite obvious the government would have to authorize a military response, as this attack was yet another in a series of rocket firing into northern Israel and a violation of the Israeli territory. The following day, the covert war between Hezbollah and Israel that had never stopped despite the 2000 Israeli withdrawal from the Lebanese territory that had been captured during the first Lebanon War in 1982, turned into a full-blown military conflict.

Israel, being such a small country, doesn't have the option to have a voluntary military service. When a country's population is about seven million citizens, and it is surrounded by countries that would rather see its demise, military service is mandatory. Furthermore, military training becomes especially useful when civilians have to face nonstop terrorist attacks. Every Israeli citizen joins the army at the age of eighteen. Women serve two years; men serve three years after which they become reservists until the age of forty-five. My husband was forty-five when the second Lebanon War started, and he was called for service as a reservist at a special medical corps unit.

He was deployed to Lebanon during the second week of the war and was part of a Forward Surgical Team (FST), which is a small mobile surgical unit that provides Level II health support in the battlefield. The surgeons in the FST units perform first aid surgeries, which allow evacuation of the wounded to a higher level of care. He called just before he crossed the border, informed me he would not have any communication means available for the following days, and made me promise I would keep the kids and myself safe.

The following weeks, alarms sounded all across the northern side of Israel, and a rain of rockets fell on Israeli cities. When sirens howled in Moshav Aviel, I rushed with my children to the ninety-six sq. ft. fortified space that is a requirement in every residential dwelling in Israel. This room has three-inch thick walls equipped with a special metal support that is capable of withstanding the blast from a missile explosion. I closed and secured the heavy iron door behind us, and we sat on the floor inside the room and waited.

"Mom, are we in danger?" Ohad asked

I glanced into his worried eyes.

"No, this is a safe room," my almost 3-year-old daughter firmly assured him.

"Yes, that's right. We are safe in here," I hugged them closer to my heart.

"Dad isn't safe, because he is outside," Gonny continued, twirling her long curly hair between her fingers.

"Dad is making sure we are fine," I said softly in a convincing tone.

A faint explosion had sounded from a distance. Later, we learned that a rocket had exploded about ten miles from us in an open area. After ten minutes, we exited the safe room, and I called my friends to make sure they were fine.

Despite the dangers, Israeli workers kept going to work. Many Israeli companies work in the global market in one way or another, and every employee knows that in order to remain a player in the business arena, we have to play like everyone else, even if that means continued operation under fire.

My husband came home for a few days, and we celebrated our daughter's third birthday early. We recorded it on our video camera, and although we didn't say anything, it was clear it could be the last documented memory we'd have. It was the saddest birthday celebration I'd ever experienced. Then, my husband left again and stayed away until a week before the month-long war ended. We spoke briefly each time before he crossed the border. I heard on the news where the fighting was taking place, and I knew he was at the heart of the combat field. Every knock on our door, every sound of a car stopping in front of our house, created a crunch in my stomach.

Finally, he came home. We didn't talk much about the war, or what he had experienced, but I knew on one occasion heavy artillery was fired toward the FST's location, prompting evacuation under fire. When I washed his uniforms, I found in one of the pockets a small, folded, dirty, yellow notepad paper. I opened it and read, "My love, life always finds a way, and you should follow it."

Life found a way, and after the war ended, our routine continued as it did before. My husband returned to the hospital, and I found a job. In the fall of 2006, I started working for a US-based computer design software company located in Needham, Massachusetts, that employs more than five thousand professionals in thirty countries around the world. The company had two research and development centers in Israel, and I worked at the Haifa office.

The design software company was one of the world's largest and fastest-growing technology companies, and I appreciated and embraced the opportunity to become a part of such a great success. I also accepted a position that was very different than anything I had done before. It wasn't a full-time position, but it involved travel as I was the academic program product specialist for the Middle East and Africa. It was an interesting position, and my manager, who was located in France, was a wonderful man who supported creativity and welcomed new initiatives. I liked the global work environment; I liked the daily communication with people from different countries and cultures. Suddenly, at work, I felt exactly where I wanted to be. I felt I belonged, and I was in the right place.

My job responsibilities included the development of partnerships and relationships with third parties, identification of key marketing opportunities, execution of an effective marketing strategy, initiation of marketing events, seminars, and development of an infrastructure for new products including training and curriculum. The thing I loved the most about my job was the level of collaboration that was needed for success. I loved my role as a member of a cross-functional, multi-cultural team, which continuously had to find ways to achieve successful operation in order to accomplish the organizational goals.

When a company operates in international markets, the understanding of the local culture is a key for success. Many times, the ability to think globally and act locally becomes a company's only competitive advantage and source for growth. In any given day, I needed to communicate with colleagues from different cultures, and every discussion needed a different set of tools, based on the culture. There were cultures I knew better than others. I didn't have any problems communicating with my American manager, who was based in France. I developed close and personal relationships with my Greek colleagues located in Athens, as my father is Greek, and I grew up in a home with a dominant Greek influence. My mom's father was Turkish, and I knew this culture pretty well, which helped me bridge the differences with my partners from Istanbul. Other cultures I knew less about, but I had the tools required to establish trust, collaboration ,and cooperation.

From a very early stage in my career, I decided I would only work for organizations with a triple bottom line that I could take pride in. Milton Friedman, the American economist, statistician, and writer, stated in a NY Times article that, "There is one and only one social responsibility of business--to use its resources and engage in activities designed to increase its profits so long as it stays within the rules of the game, which is to say, engages in open and free competition without deception or fraud." I agree that business' first priority is to make a profit, but I disagree there is one and only one social responsibility of business. For me the bottom line, or the triple Ps—Profit, People, Planet—should coexist in every business. A business that solely focuses on profit should cease to exist, as it ruptures the delicate embroidery of its ecosystem, which depends on it.

The academic program I worked for was a brilliant example of the incredible contribution of a business to society, while making a profit. The academic program supported institutions by providing free design, calculation, and collaboration software to K-12 educational programs. The company also donated computer labs, curriculum, and training programs. It was clear the donation was a long-term investment, and that at some point in time, the generations of students who were trained on the software may become its users in their future work places, but in a business world that bows and prays to short-term investments, the academic program was unique and innovative.

Three months after I had started working for the academic program, I traveled to Manchester, UK, for training purposes, and I used this opportunity to meet with my manager, who was in the city for business. We met for dinner at the hotel restaurant, and we talked about the goals that I had to meet and the challenges I faced. I had an idea about the quality of work I was delivering, but he caught me by surprise when he offered me a promotion and asked me to consider taking responsibility for Eastern Europe.

The addition of Eastern Europe to my daily schedule would have many ramifications. I would need to increase my hours and switch to a full-time position. The region needed a lot of support as an infrastructure barely existed, which required the formation of relationships and the development of a foundation for the new establishment. This would dramatically increase my business travel time that was already active without adding more. I realized the initial investment in Eastern Europe would be consuming in both time and resources, would come at the expense of the region I was already responsible for, and my personal life.

I was proud to be offered the promotion, and I enjoyed the vote of confidence from my manager, but I wasn't naïve. I was already familiar with the route from job to career, and I knew the toll required. I knew if I were to accept the job, I would soon have to find a surrogate mommy for my toddler daughter and my seven-year-old son. I would have to give up supporting my son's literacy work and hire someone to do it for me. I couldn't imagine someone else that would be as devoted to the cause as I was.

My husband was working non-stop as a transplant surgeon. All three transplant units operating in Israel were very active. We never knew what to expect. Every dinner party we threw, every birthday we celebrated, every family gathering, every weekend during the five years we lived in Israel was interrupted at least once, let alone the ordinary days with the rare family time in which his pager would beep, after which he was gone for the next twenty-four hours.

When I started working for the academic program and needed to travel, I could never rely on my husband to hold the reins, unless he used vacation days to stay home. I always created a weird arrangement for the kids. I didn't experience any peace of mind during my travels; I was more worried about all the things that could go wrong at home than I was about a meeting going badly or a plane crashing. My only comfort was the time difference was insignificant, and I could take care of problems in real time.

I remember a phone call I received from my son's school administrator prior to an important meeting I was having with academic executives from all over Athens at the office of my Greek partner. The administrator informed me no one had arrived to pick up my son. I was the second speaker at the meeting, and I had hoped to have a few more minutes to go over my speech. Instead, I made a few calls and found someone who could pick up my son. When I went into the room, I opened my speech by talking about the importance of finding creative solutions to burning problems and related it to the software solutions my company offered to K-12 grades in the various educational programs. Needless to say, this introduction was nowhere in my notes for the talk.

After a week of soul searching, or better yet, resolution searching, I realized I wasn't ready to pay the extremely high price two careers would entail. I hoped in a few years, a solution would be found to my husband's work schedule. I wanted my children to grow up with the values and principles that I instilled in them, not a nanny's. I trusted my own judgment, because I knew my children's individual personalities very well. I thought in a few years, I would pursue a career, and I'd be better than ever at it, because I would not feel guilty or tormented for choosing to go against my values and instincts. I notified my manager I could not accept the promotion. I increased my work hours, but I didn't take full responsibility for Eastern Europe.

Six months after the war, we faced the same difficulties as before, but our perspective had changed, and suddenly, our family's wellbeing was the spotlight. It wasn't about my career, his career, a proper dyslexia therapy, the financial situation, and security; it was all of those things wrapped together into a small rubber-band ball that bounced all over our reality and forced us to think about a solution.

It became clear the department of surgery at the hospital in Jerusalem, under the leadership of the current chairman, was ill fated. However, the chairman wasn't going anywhere. My husband could resign and again look for a position in one of the other two transplantation units in Israel. One of the units wasn't hiring, and the second didn't offer any financial incentives. They were willing to hire him, but his salary would be modest, and he could not pursue private care as a way to increase his income. Also, he would still have to work around the clock in the highly-demanding field of transplantation surgery.

Meanwhile, the director of transplantation surgery left, and my husband was nominated as the interim director of the unit. He had all the responsibilities and liabilities that came with the job, but his employment conditions remained the same. He received the same careless attitude, was presented with the same last-minute yearly contract, and didn't have a prospect of tenure. He didn't get an office, didn't have access to private health care to improve his income, and he dedicated countless of hours to work at the expense of our family time.

We had long conversations during which we considered our options. I didn't see a way to resume my career as long as my husband was engaged in transplantation surgery, at least not until the kids were much older. I couldn't come to terms with the fact my son wasn't getting the proper dyslexia therapy, and I certainly didn't accept the fact he would not be able to learn English, a must-have expertise in today's world. I wasn't willing to accept that after a self-paid fellowship in a highly-regarded surgical specialization, we still needed to ask our parents for financial support. I was tired of conflicts, and I wanted some peace.

After several years of feeling displaced, suddenly my husband also shared my emotions, and the wildest way out—the one that we'd never considered applicable or even attainable—came to be the one we followed.

18

THE END OF AN ERA

*I*n 2007, almost a year after the war, the academic department at the company I worked for shut down in Israel, and the management of Eastern Europe, the Middle East, and Africa was taken over by the European office. I started looking for a new job that would enable me to resume my career. My husband and I agreed it was impossible for me to pursue a career while his career was highly demanding and the children were so young. His salary was insufficient to support our family's needs, and the cost of living was very high. He decided to look for a second fellowship that would complement his first in organ transplantation, and one that could coexist with my career.

He was, and still is, an incredible diagnostician and a gifted surgeon, and he believed a fellowship in surgical oncology would allow him to provide an excellent standard of care for his patients. Very few surgeons pursue a second fellowship, and having two fellowships that complement each other the way transplantation surgery and surgical oncology do would have granted him a unique competitive advantage. He started applying for a fellowship in the United States.

The years after the second Lebanon War were far from easy, comfortable, or painless. It seemed like everything was an effort, and nothing was simple. I accepted a part-time job as a marketing manager for a small software company that developed Geographic Information System solutions and civil engineering Computer-Aided Design products. The company sold its products both domestically and internationally, and I believed in its potential to grow. The position was a step forward from the position I'd held previously. I was responsible for the communications and marketing materials, including the maintenance of the company's website.

The job allowed me to follow a career path, support my son's dyslexia remediation, and my family. I loved the fact the company was small and had never employed a marketing manager before. I worked in an open space that was loud, my cubical was small, and so was my marketing budget, but I was grateful to have been given a unique opportunity to build something from scratch and make a difference. I enjoyed the challenges I faced, and I was pleased to work again in the global environment. The company presented its products at international fairs, and I was responsible for the exhibitions.

Yet, when I was home helping my son to achieve proficiency in reading and writing, I couldn't help but notice he was far behind his grade level, and he needed more help than I could ever offer. He still worked with his private teacher at school, but she was not a Dyslexia therapy specialist. I read about the ways Dyslexia therapy was being conducted in the United States, and about the astonishing progress children with Dyslexia had shown by following a dedicated Dyslexia therapy program. I read the research and explored the assistive technology solutions that were available in classrooms and at home to children in the United States, which were far better than anything I could find in Israel.

My son's dedication, commitment, and determination to gain literacy were extraordinary; however, it broke my heart to know there was a better way for him to overcome his difficulties, but it wasn't available.

My husband came home one day and told me he had seen a transplant surgeon, that he'd recognized from the surgical community, walking down the hallway toward the hospital's administration office. My husband was familiar with the fact this physician's reputation was stained. Despite the fact my husband was the interim director of the transplantation unit, his chairman had never talked with him about the future of his position. My husband had a feeling the physician he had seen was coming for an interview for the position of the transplant unit director.

It was 2008, and for the last two years, my husband had sought a fellowship in surgical oncology without success. Each year since 2005, I had applied for the United States green card lottery with no luck. But I was not ready to stop trying. I didn't know what the future held, but I knew t giving up was not an option. There must be a way, a solution, and a chance for a better future.

A few months later, my husband had a performance evaluation meeting with his chairman, during which he asked for a permanent nomination, but he was informed the physician who had come for an interview had been nominated as the director of the unit. My husband was devastated, and for weeks, I watched him walking around defeated and tormented.

It was the fall of 2008, and the mood around the house was somber, just as the weather outside. Was that all there was?

We desperately needed a break from everything, to get away for a little while, and just breathe. We asked our parents to watch over the kids, and we flew out to where I felt I belonged, to where I felt a better future was possible.

We landed at JFK and took a taxi to our long-time American friends' apartment in Chelsea. From the second I landed, I felt free and happy. We reached the city, and I was in my Manhattan—my noisy, unclean, neurotic, hectic, extravagant, never-stopping metropolis where I felt comfortable.

After a couple of days, we traveled to Boston for a long weekend. From all the places I have visited in the fall nowhere compares to New England. The air is cool and crisp, the trees show off their most magnificent-colored foliage, farmers present their giant pumpkins on tables on the sides of roads, and nature in the late afternoon light can convert the most cynical person in the world to a pantheist.

On our way to Boston, we stopped at a small bakery for apple cider doughnuts and hot tea, returned to our rented car, opened all four windows, and listened to Chet Baker plays *Almost Blue* on his trumpet. It was 4 pm and the leaves were scarlet, persimmon, maroon, olive, and gold, and New England's rivers and ponds looked like Leonid Afremov oil paintings. Our noses were red, my hair was blowing in the wind, my husband was humming Chet's tunes, and after a long time, I remembered how pleasant harmony feels.

When we arrived in Boston, we turned off our phones, and we didn't have any online connection. We enjoyed the quiet time, and we walked around the city, like two teenagers with no commitments. Four days later, we returned to Manhattan, and I was sitting with Christine on the balcony sharing a laugh, when my husband who was checking his email on the computer calmly said, "I think I've got a surgical oncology fellowship offer from Memorial Sloan Kettering for the summer."

Christine and I jumped off our chairs and stormed inside. "What do you mean You Think?" we inquired at the same time.

"There are two letters of offer from Memorial's administrative office in my mailbox. The first has a different name in the greeting line, but it was recalled. The second has my name." He revolved the screen and showed us.

Todd and Christine took charge, and after careful consideration, Christine announced, "Welcome back!"

"I believe this is my cue to finally open the Louis Roederer Cristal Brut I received from a client a couple of weeks ago." Todd winked at us and went to the kitchen.

Christine and I hugged for a long moment, while Todd poured the bubbly champagne into the tall crystal flutes; we raised our glasses and toasted, "To the future."

It was Monday, November 3, 2008—a day before the elections, and America was on its way to making history. Could we make our own little history as well? Had a window finally opened for us? It was the opportunity we had wished for, and we were not willing to let it go to waste. I couldn't fall asleep, and I stayed up, thinking for most of the night.

On Tuesday, November 4, 2008, the 56th quadrennial presidential election took place, and America made history when it elected its first black president. On Wednesday, Americans woke up to a genuine change, maybe the greatest change for decades. There was a feeling of promise in the air, of a new era where color is only a spectrum of light, and anyone could reach farther than his or her own dreams. Although I was only an observer, I felt how infectious and inspiring the feeling of hope was. People should consider themselves very lucky to have experienced the magnitude of such hope in their lifetime. Many people live and die without it.

I was filled with hope and anticipation when my husband called the administration office at Memorial Sloan Kettering. We were invited to the office to pick up paperwork and learn about the housing arrangements and schools around the neighborhood. On Thursday, we toured our future apartment and met with the school's principal. On Friday, we were on the plane heading back home.

There are really no words that can accurately describe the way we felt. Our break from everything that wasn't working transformed into an opportunity for a better future. We were excited, hopeful, and motivated all at the same time. It felt as if all of a sudden there were no limits, just open plains stretching all the way to the horizon. It felt as if our future was a blank page that had left the paper-mill and was ready to be written upon. It was a chance for a new beginning, a better beginning, and a more promising beginning.

We decided to keep the news a secret until we had figured out what our next move would be. Memorial Sloan Kettering arranged for a J visa for my husband; once again, we were required to leave after the end of the fellowship, which was expected to be for a year, but there was one crucial difference. I'd already paid the price of leaving everything behind when I joined my husband on his journey to self-fulfillment back in 2001. It was not in my plans to repeat it. We must find a way to stay in the United States.

For me, this repositioning was really the beginning of an immigration process. I figured the immigration route would be many things, but not easy. We weren't refugees, we didn't need an asylum, we didn't have family members who were United States citizens, and the future employer could not ask for a permanent residency for us because it was a one-year fellowship without an employment commitment. We were only two highly-skilled professionals who were able to inject valuable skills into the United States economy and actively contribute to the society.

Yet I knew that by the end of the fellowship, my husband would have gained a competitive advantage that only a handful of physicians in the field had. He would have two fellowships in highly-esteemed specialties in surgery from two world-leading medical institutions. I hoped it would be enough to open doors that otherwise would have been closed. I believed there would be a way to waive the J-1 visa two-year requirement to return to the country of last residence for two years before applying for any other visa, and we would be allowed to stay in the United States.

March 1st was the new transplant unit director's first day at work. My husband walked into the office of the chairman of the department of surgery and notified him he would be leaving the hospital at the end of his contract in June.

"Where are you headed?" the chairman asked with a condescending smirk.

"You may know this hospital, Memorial Sloan Kettering, New York," My husband simply replied, and then he exited the room, leaving the chairman behind with his mouth wide open.

A few years later, the hospital in Jerusalem where my husband had worked, declared bankruptcy after getting three-hundred-seventy million dollars in debt and needing a government bailout. It was hardly a surprise.

During the time of my husband's employment, the leadership was inefficient, suffered from a lack of humility, empathy, and vision, and believed it could outsmart the system. Under this leadership, senior doctors could legally use hospital resources to provide services to private patients, and sometimes even during the workday when they were supposed to provide public medical services for which they were paid. The institution didn't apply a sustainable business model, which caused doctors to pocket most of the profits, at the expense of the hospital.

Although the leadership was well aware of the hospital's shaky financial situation, it followed its plans to build a new admission tower, spending three-hundred-sixty-three million dollars, knowing the upkeep of the facility would be expensive, and increase significantly the operating budget. Big egos, power plays, internal competition, self-satisfaction, and self-indulgence can never yield success and growth. They can only lead to demise.

The months prior to our move to the United States were busy, because in our minds it wasn't just a one-year relocation, it was immigration. We evaluated our options, and figured the future we wished for was not within reach in Israel. Moreover, the relocation to New York in 2001 had opened a whole new world for me, which continued to take shape while I was back in Israel. For me, it was a simple understanding I didn't necessarily have to live my life where I grew up.

My state of mind could be compared to someone who was born in Florida, went to college in Connecticut, and decided to settle down in New York. However, for me, it was moving between countries, not states. I considered the future move to New York the same way I had previously regarded the return to Israel; I was going back to a familiar place. The last eight years were full of transitions, and I stopped regarding them as hurdles. They became natural for me. I was an expatriate, a repatriate, and I frequently traveled for work to different countries. The world literally became my small village. I felt I had never stopped learning. Every new encounter filled my being with knowledge and new insights. I wasn't intimidated by change. I was challenged by change, and I loved it.

We took a great risk in putting our house on the market and shipping everything we had overseas, knowing our visa was only authorized for one year, after which we would have to return to our last place of residence. However, the cost to stay in Israel and compromise our future justified the risk.

I realized that in life you can only regret something you did, not something you hadn't done. I took regret into consideration and decided I could live with disappointment, but I could not live with defeat.

It wasn't easy to share our decision to immigrate to the United States with our family and friends. Some didn't understand why we could not just accept reality, lower our expectations, and stay in our country. I guess if we had not become expatriates once, we would have probably been asking the same questions. However, relocation can influence people in different ways. You can either relocate, repatriate and feel like nothing has ever happened, or you can change forever, or something in between.

I changed forever, soaked everything in and completely assimilated with the new culture. I was never afraid to lose my identity, and it allowed me to accept an additional one. I was able to view possibilities for lifestyles, values and norms, and I was ready to incorporate them into my life. I figured out what I wanted, and eventually, I followed my heart.

On June 16th, 2009, we got on the plane to New York. Our journey had just begun.

19

THE VISA GAMES

The relocation to Manhattan in the summer of 2009 was nothing like the one in 2001. I was already familiar with the culture and language, the norms, values, and social cues. I knew what to expect from the city. I had left my job, but I had not lost myself. I was the same person, only without a job or a career. I was focused and determined, and already pursuing my goal to find a better future in the United States.

I believed a solution to the visa requirement would be found, and we would not have to go back to our country at the end of the fellowship. I was ready to make compromises as long as a solution was granted. There was one thing I wasn't ready to do—go back. Never in my life had I felt so certain that reverse would involve repentance.

We lived on the corner of 66th Street and York Avenue in the MSKCC's housing, just across the street from the hospital. My husband went straight to work, but this time, he wasn't a surgical resident, but an established transplant surgeon with five years' experience in performing complex operations, diagnostics, and intricate decisions. He was somewhat familiar with surgical oncology and anticipated the opportunity to expand his knowledge and enhance his skills.

I enrolled the kids in a public school that was located on our block and required only a five minute walk from the apartment. Public School 183 was located near the triangle of Cornell Medical Center, Rockefeller University, and Memorial Sloan Kettering Cancer Center, which made it the most diverse school I had ever seen, as it proudly accommodated students from sixty-eight countries. The school adopted a child-centered approach to meet the needs of individual students, and used its diversity as a leverage to gain access to resources that would ensure high-quality instruction.

Prior to the first day of school, I met with the academic and administrative staff during which I discussed my son's Dyslexia and the ramifications of our relocation on his learning process. I came prepared with a linguistic evaluation translated into English, and letters from his teachers that contained important information about previous accommodations and teaching techniques that had proven to be successful. I was thrilled to hear what the school had to offer and how professional the team was. We scheduled a language evaluation for the second week of school, followed by a meeting with the English Second Language educators, and the fourth grade teachers.

The school had a special needs class for each grade level with no more than fifteen students in it, and two Special Education teachers. Additionally, in many of the classrooms, there was an assistant, funded by the PTA. The assistant handled most of the issues that were time consuming and freed the teachers to focus on the children's varied needs.

From the start, it was noticeable the challenges ahead of us were bigger than anything we could have anticipated. My son had to do almost the impossible and acquire literacy skills in a second language before they were even established in his first language. The school was completely engaged in the task ahead and on top of the ESL sessions. The special needs class included my son in a unique program that was available through the school. The program was based on a collaboration between Hunter College and the school, in which Special Education master's students provided private lessons at no cost to students with learning disabilities, as part of their practice requirements. My son was assigned to a master's student who was an ESL and Special Education teacher with eight years' experience in the classroom. He stayed twice a week after school to study with her.

My daughter was a different story. She started first grade at PS 183 and was very excited to learn English as a second language. She used to watch my son's children's movies, which were mostly in English, a permanent reminder of our first relocation to New York. After the first month of school, I asked her if she had made any new friends, to which she logically responded, "I don't have friends, because I don't speak the language; when I do, I can have as many friends as I wish." And so she did. After six months, she spoke English and had a few friends.

I was having the time of my life. I strolled for hours in the city, with a smile on my face, especially each time I arrived in Central Park. I visited my favorite museums like the Frick Collection and the Museum of Arts and Design. I attended special exhibitions at the Met and the Whitney, and I didn't skip significant showcases at the Prada Museum, Cartier Gallery, the Louis Vuitton Institution, or the Chanel Academy. I went to daytime movies and Broadway matinees with Nadine who was the wife of the MSKCC's second international fellow who arrived from Germany. Nadine and I went shopping together, and I introduced her to my favorite restaurants like Republic, Dawat, Maya, and Hummus Place. Manhattan had remained just as I remembered it, and I loved it even more.

The first few months in Manhattan were pleasant and satisfying. My husband enjoyed his fellowship, the children were getting the support they needed to overcome the challenges they faced, and I felt like I belonged. For the first time in six years, I was exactly where I wanted to be.

Medical fellows usually start looking for a job during the winter of their final year of a fellowship, and so did my husband. But unlike his American colleagues, he was not American board certified, he was not a citizen, and he hadn't completed all of the three-step examinations required for medical licensure in the United States. However, unlike the vast majority of the

American transplant surgeons, he had a fellowship in surgical oncology, and unlike the vast majority of the American surgical oncologists, he had a fellowship in transplantation surgery. The two fellowships not only complemented each other, but they allowed my husband to provide a superior standard of care, take on cases other surgical oncologists would consider too risky, experience fewer complications, and discharge patients rather quickly after surgery.

It was not surprising that soon after he had applied for surgical oncology positions in leading medical institutions, most of them contacted him immediately. He had job offers from Los Angeles, Philadelphia, Syracuse, and Seattle, but his J-1 visa required us to go back to Israel at the end of the fellowship. We needed to consult with an immigration lawyer regarding our options.

Todd, our old-time friend, was a lawyer, and he happened to know an immigration attorney whom we had scheduled to meet just before the holidays.

We took the elevator to the eighteenth floor of an office building on 3rd Avenue. The receptionist guided us to the attorney's traditionally designed office that smelled of old lumber, and overlooked the Art Deco-terraced crown of the Chrysler Building. We sat in the espresso-colored rich leather, brass nail head-decorated club chairs, and had about three seconds to feel comfortable before the lawyer announced, "You're in a complicated situation."

"This is because I have a J-1 visa, which compels us to return to our country for a minimum of two years once my training was completed." My husband nodded in agreement.

"That is correct. If you wish to stay in the United States, first, you must agree to practice in, or serve in, a federally designated medically underserved area of a state for a period of three years. Second, you would need to change your visa status to O-1A or H-1B, and only after the three years of service in an underserved area could you apply for a permanent residency," he explained the situation briefly.

We knew what a medically underserved area was. It was a place in which the population-to-provider ratio indicates a shortage. These areas cannot attract enough skilled physicians to provide the necessary medical services. Obviously, there are many reasons for physicians to avoid underserved areas—some are financial, some are personal, and some are professional. A surgeon who goes through medical school, residency, and fellowship has invested an average of thirteen years to become a skilled professional, after which he or she expects to receive some return on the investment. It doesn't necessarily have to be a monetary return, but it should be a type of return, like practice in an established hospital, working in a service that cultivates research and personal development, or just residing in a place where the spouse can find a job, or the children can have access to a fine education. A medically underserved area, to a surgical oncologist who wishes to work in a university hospital, means the location suffers from a wide range of deficiencies.

"We took into account the fact we would need to live in the middle of nowhere before we could live somewhere. How can we overcome the J-1 condition that requires us to go back to Israel for two years before we can apply for a different type of visa?" I asked.

"You will have to change your visa status, and you have two options available. You could change the status to H-1B or O-1A. The H-1B visa is a non-immigrant visa that allows US companies to employ foreign workers in specialty occupations that require expertise in specialized fields. You are a foreign physician, which means you will need to receive a medical licensure in the United States. To receive a license, you will have to pass the USMLE, United States Medical Licensing Examination, a three-step examination." He clarified.

"You know, the USMLE three-step examination is equal to the ones I have already taken during my residency in Israel. In order to successfully pass the exams, I need to study for them as they cover the basic medical and scientific principles essential for effective health care, and comprehensive knowledge of health and disease in the context of patient management. The wait time for taking the exams is long, and I don't think I will be able to give everything I have to the fellowship, study for, and take the exams before the end of the fellowship in June," my husband said, sadly, and took a long sip of his water.

"In this case, you are left with one option. You could apply for the O-1A visa. The O-1A visa is a non-immigrant temporary worker visa granted to individuals with an extraordinary ability in the sciences, education, business, or athletics that come to the United States to continue working in the area of their extraordinary ability. The visa is initially granted for up to three years, but can be extended for one year at a time."

"Could you tell us more about the O-1A visa?" I asked.

"According to the USCIS, an individual who applies for an O-1A visa should present evidence he or she has received a major, internationally-recognized award, such as a Nobel Prize, or evidence of at least three items on a list of eight extraordinary achievements. The list includes items such as receipt of a nationally or internationally-recognized prize or award for excellence in the field of endeavor, original scientific, scholarly, or business-related contributions of major significance in the field, authorship of scholarly articles in professional journals or other major media in the field for which classification is sought, and a high salary or other remuneration for services as evidenced by contracts or other reliable evidence, among others. From everything you have told me, you could easily fit into at least four extraordinary achievements. After your fellowship, you will be what one out of maybe four physicians in the USA with such credentials and experience? If that isn't extraordinary, then I don't know what is," the lawyer said with a grin, and continued before we were able to respond.

"Keep in mind the O-1A status, unlike the H-1B, does not have a route to permanent residency, and in order to later apply for permanent residency, you would have to change the status again, this time to H-1B. The spouse is not allowed to work either with O-1A or H-1B. Additionally, every time you change your visa status, you must be present at an American consulate outside the US, preferably in your home country. Therefore, you will have to bear the costs related to traveling to Israel and applying for a new visa at least three times over the next three years. " He finally concluded.

We thanked the attorney, left his office, and silently walked towards the elevator while processing the information we'd just heard. It was one of those times, in which my experience as a system analyst and project manager came in handy; otherwise, it would have taken me probably months to process all the facts. I immediately drew a flowchart in my head containing all the steps and boxes of various kinds, just like a computer algorithm with the entire flow including all of the yes's, no's, if's, and but's. However, unlike a computer algorithm, it didn't have any logic.

We exited the building, holding hands, and walked until we arrived at Katharine Hepburn Garden in Dag Hammarskjöld Plaza, where we sat on a damp bench.

I was upset. "I cannot understand why an individual that America considers to be extraordinary should go through such torment," I said. "If a person has a Nobel Prize or other internationally-recognized award, why on earth does someone who is *that* extraordinary receive a visa that limits his or her stay in the United States and that does not provide the spouse a work authorization? If an individual is so unique, and wishes to make an extraordinary contribution to the United States, why wouldn't he be accepted with open arms and invited to stay in America? I suppose there is a limit to how many extraordinary individuals a nation can generate from within," I loudly and cynically asserted.

"True, and even more senseless is the fact that I will have to serve in an underserved area. O-1A visa means that America thinks I am an extraordinary surgeon, but instead of having a surgeon who can perform an exclusive type of cancer operations in densely populated locations where I am needed the most, I'm being sent to a rural location with a community hospital at best. In those areas, I might not have the operation room services that are needed to support the surgeries I perform, so although I'm highly qualified, so qualified that I'm considered extraordinary, I cannot do what I do best." He looked away with a somber expression.

"It's terrible you have offers from leading cancer centers, but you have to wait for a job opening in an underserved area," I said.

"You know that either of the visa statuses, whether it is H or O, would allow only me to work in the United States. You and the kids are eligible to apply for a non-immigrant visa that may allow you to engage in full or part-time study, but not to be employed." My husband was concerned.

"Yes, I understand but once again, I am puzzled by the immigration system that denies a highly-skilled spouse the option to contribute to the American economy, and intentionally draws professionals out of the market-place, as needed as they might be. I could have been a perfect fit for so many companies." I gazed at the tall Christmas tree under the iron gazebo.

When I looked back at my husband, I saw a man in his mid-forties, who was willing to start over. He was ready to repeat two of the most extensive examinations in medicine, finish a second fellowship, turn down both lucrative and exclusive positions in leading medical institutions, and instead reside and work in a medically underserved area in the middle of nowhere with all of the consequences that implied. But instead of thinking about him, he was worried about my situation. He was bothered by the fact I would not be able to work.

Soft tiny drops of rain started to fall around us. I met his eyes and held his hands, guiding him from the bench. "Tsach, we are in this as one. A better future comes with an expensive price tag, we knew that, but it will pay off," I said with a cheerful smile.

It started drizzling as he leaned down, removed a stray hair from my lips, pulled me close, and kissed me—a tender, long kiss. "I must run back to work, we'll talk later," he murmured, pressing my cold hands between his, and then hurried up the street.

I opened my bright yellow umbrella with the words *sunshine on a cloudy day* and walked to the nearest subway station. The train arrived, and I sat down by the doors in the middle of an almost-empty car, stared at an ad sponsored by a Protestant church that read, "Because Some Answers Aren't Found On Google," and couldn't agree more.

I thought about everything I had heard from the lawyer. I realized it would be possible to stay in the United States if my husband would be willing to take step two and step three of the medical examinations, and we needed to be willing to reside in an underserved area and be willing to first change our visa status to O, then to H, and wait three years to apply for a permanent residency, with each visa status change requiring travel to the American consulate in our country—and if I would be willing to be unemployed for at least the next four years, depending on how fast the changes in visa status would be.

When I exited the subway station, the skies had cleared, and a smooth stream of sunlight gently stroked my face and followed me all the way to our building. I closed the door behind me, sat on my bed, and watched the Roosevelt Island Tramway's vivid red cable car gliding above the East River, slowly making its way towards Manhattan.

I thought about the conversation I once had with Ruthie about options, and I remembered having options is one of the most critical components of the decision-making process. We had a couple of options. We could go back to Israel at the end of the fellowship, wait two years during which my husband could take the two steps of the USMLE, and apply for H visa that would not allow me to work, but at least we could apply for a green card after a short period of time. The risk with this option was that it would be harder, or even impossible, to find an attending position while residing in another country. The second option was to follow the attorney's advice and choose the route he had depicted.

When people consider their options, they rarely choose the craziest one on the list. Why would they? Most of the time, options that may not be the best will still be good enough to follow, and options that are plain crazy will not even be worth the time invested in the decision-making process. But what do you do when the craziest option is the most promising one? Is it worth following?

Over the next few days, I explained the situation to our families and friends, and I told them we had decided to do whatever was necessary to immigrate to the United States. My ecosystem didn't think the route to stay in the United States made any sense. We were two skilled professionals, who could easily find jobs in any country, and make a significant contribution to the community and the economy. They didn't understand why it had to be the United States, if other countries would not only welcome us, but would support us in various ways.

They didn't understand why I would choose to stay unemployed. In 2010, two years after the financial crisis, America exhibited a 9.6 percent unemployment rate, the highest in decades, and I didn't think I could find an employer willing to change my visa status in order to hire me. Mostly, my friends and family didn't understand why we would choose to live in an underserved area, give up many important advantages such as education, professional possibilities, entertainment, and basically our lifestyle, just to find out later that it would be even harder to find a job when we exited such a place.

I was unable to explain rationally why we chose to follow the option that made less sense than any other. I believe most people who are gifted with the ability to have a vision and follow their wildest dreams cannot logically explain their actions. They visualize where they want to be and create or follow a path that allows them to get there. They encounter hardships, obstacles, and many difficulties, but they are persistent and determined to succeed. Without these kinds of people, we wouldn't have the science, technology, medicine, arts, and values we enjoy and are thankful for today.

I had a modest vision. I saw America as our best bet for a better future. I preferred to compromise for a few years, rather than return to Israel and compromise for a lifetime. We decided to follow the path that would eventually grant us permanent residency.

The job offers my husband received were from leading institutions, the types of institutions that every physician would have welcomed the opportunity to work for. They were disappointed to hear my husband would not be able to accept the offer, because the hospital was not located in an underserved area. They needed a surgeon with my husband's credentials, and only a handful of surgical oncologists in the United States had such credentials. The implications of hiring highly-qualified surgeons are all-encompassing and go beyond monetary considerations.

Highly-qualified surgeons have the ability to influence and inspire generations of residents and medical students. Those surgeons promote best practices, which improve the quality and safety of health care. They provide a superior standard of care, help reduce the patient admission time, and significantly decrease the readmission rate to the benefit of both the patients and the hospital.

My husband needed to wait for an offer from an underserved area, or leave the United States at the end of the fellowship.

After a few weeks, I felt at peace with the fact I could not work for at least four years. Yet, although the O and the H visa restricted my ability to work, they didn't limit my ability to grow, prove myself, or be proud of myself. I decided those four years would be meaningful and would add value to my life more than any job I could have.

20

RUNNING AGAINST TIME

At the beginning of 2010, my husband received a job offer from an underserved area; it was a surgical oncologist position at the University of New Mexico Cancer Center in Albuquerque, New Mexico. All we knew about America at that time had been formed by our introduction to the east coast. We loved exploring new places, and, during the times we had lived in New York, we traveled all the way north to Canada and south to Florida, including Washington D.C., and many other interesting places along the way. However, we had never gone west, and we didn't know what to expect. As a matter of fact, when my husband told me he had a job offer, he said it was in Abercrombie, NM—to give you an idea of what east coasters we were.

When my husband returned from his first interview, he was dazed and slightly confused by the city. Albuquerque is a high-altitude city located in the central part of New Mexico, on both sides of the Rio Grande River that flows from south central Colorado to the Gulf of Mexico. It was a medically underserved area, but it was anything but a godforsaken place. It was an enchanted, spiritual, unworldly place—the kind of place that takes your breath away. From all of the medically underserved areas, it was probably the best place we could land, as Albuquerque is far from being deserted; it is the home of more than 600,000 people, and ranks as the thirty-second-largest city in the United States.

However, Albuquerque suffers from many deficiencies that make it unappealing to highly-skilled professionals. The city has approximately seven hundred manufacturing firms, but has almost no high-tech industry. The education system is insufficient, to say the least. The city struggles with a high crime rate, hunger, poverty, and gun violence. The university hospital's surgical oncology division was established a few years prior to our arrival, but was completely dysfunctional until a new chief was hired and started shaping it into what it has become today. He was desperately searching for a highly-skilled surgical oncologist with a specialty in liver, pancreas, bile duct, and gallbladder surgery, and when my husband showed interest in the position, he could not have been more grateful. He had searched for a suitable surgeon for over a year.

Not only was my husband a skilled surgeon, he also had five years' experience in transplantation surgery, one of those years as the interim director of a transplant unit, two fellowships from two different, world-leading medical institutions, and an enthusiastic recommendation from the head of the division of general surgical oncology at Memorial Sloan Kettering, naming him in the top ten percent of the best fellows who had served there.

Yet, my husband had to take two examinations to obtain an American medical license, and he needed to apply for a change in his visa status. The university hospital in New Mexico was determined to hire him and connected us with an immigration lawyer that would help with the process of changing our status from a non-immigrant to permanent residency. My husband had enough evidence to match the criteria for an O-1A visa, as he had extraordinary ability in his field. Parallel to the legal procedures, he had started to study for his exams.

The Step 2 USMLE's Clinical Knowledge is a one-day examination, and graduates of medical schools located outside the US and Canada need to apply through the Educational Commission for Foreign Medical Graduates' website. The Step 2 CK can be taken in one of five evaluation centers located across the United States. My husband's fellowship was very active, and on top of it, he had to study for two major examinations. So I took charge of the process and did what I knew best. I became our household's project manager.

When I first tried to find a center and schedule a date for the exam, there were no appointments available until August. We were running against time. I started looking for test appointments' cancellations that usually occurred a day or two prior to the exam, which left almost no time for planning. Some days, there were no cancellations in any of the centers, on other days there were maybe one or two, but I needed to constantly sit by the computer to apply for them immediately.

After a couple of weeks, I recognized that when an exam slot became available, it took less than a minute for it to be captured by another applicant. Each of the five centers had their own scheduling webpage, so by the time I had browsed from one center's screen to another, a vacant slot was long gone. I downloaded an application that refreshed the screen every five seconds, minimized the five screens in a way that I could see them all at once, and applied instantly when a slot became available.

One morning, after dropping off the kids at school, I arrived at the apartment, and from a distance, on the laptop screen, I noticed the purple square that indicated a vacant slot on the calendar of the Houston, TX evaluation center. I sprinted to the computer, clicked on the purple square, and applied for the exam that was scheduled for the next morning. Straight away, I booked a noon flight and texted my husband, "Good morning, you have a flight to Houston in three hours; the exam is scheduled for tomorrow morning."

Then I booked a hotel nearby the center, ordered a taxi pickup service to JFK, and packed his duffel bag. He came home an hour later, took his luggage, and left for the car that was waiting for him by the building. A few minutes later, he texted me, "You are the best, Miss Moneypenny," to which I replied, "Flattery will get you nowhere, James...but don't stop trying."

In April, after the second examination, we crossed our fingers the USCIS would approve our new visa status before the end of the fellowship. The lawyer raced against time and submitted an expedited request for an O-1A. It was the beginning of June, and we still hadn't heard anything from the immigration office. We had to leave the United States within thirty days after the end of the fellowship. We needed to vacate our apartment at the end of June, and we didn't know whether to pack and send our belongings to Albuquerque, New Mexico, or to Tel Aviv, Israel.

If the immigration office had questions or needed clarifications, it might take a few months before we would be approved for a visa change. We were both extremely worried and, in addition to the fellowship duties, my husband had to study for the last exam of the American medical licensure that was considered the most challenging. He was scheduled to take the exam a day after the end of the fellowship.

On June 4th, we received the USCIS approval for a change in our visa status. At that moment, my husband was acknowledged as extraordinary, not only by his mother, but by the United States of America. The two-day USMLE exam took place on July 1st and 2nd, after which we traveled to the airport on our way to Israel to change our visa status at the American consulate. At the airport, my husband received a phone call from the University Hospital of New Mexico.

He swayed slightly on his feet while he spoke on the phone, his expression guarded. After the call had ended, he gazed at me, took a deep breath, and said, "It was the administrator, and she told me there were two problems that could prevent me from receiving a New Mexico medical license. The first problem is I have more than a seven-year gap between the first stage of the medical examination and the second and third. This could be solved by retaking the first stage of the USMLE. The second problem is that the medical board of New Mexico requires at least two years of an accredited residency education program, and I have only one."

"Yes, but you have three years of fellowships. A fellowship is a specialty program you undertake after completing a residency program, which means any American institution that hires you assumes you have the experience that is needed for an advanced training." I attempted to defend his position.

"My fellowships, exceptional as they may be, are not considered to be accredited programs, as they were not a residency but advanced training. Many medical boards across the United States do not have such requirements, because it only makes sense that advanced training is superior to a residency. However, that is not the case in New Mexico, and this problem doesn't have a solution," my husband said with a sigh.

The news created even more stress in the nerve-wracking reality we had lived in for months. Yet giving up now wasn't an option. We flew to Israel, changed our visa status at the American consulate, and wrote a letter to the Director of the Medical Board of New Mexico, and to the Governor of New Mexico. The University Hospital in Albuquerque did the same, backing up the need to change the medical licensure requirements in New Mexico. The hospital argued the city is considered a medically underserved area, and although it has a designated cancer center, it is extremely hard to attract highly-skilled professionals. As a result, patients had to travel out-of-state to seek medical treatment.

New Mexico takes one of the top spots for poorest state in the nation, and many patients who cannot afford medical treatment away from home are left without any treatment. Additionally, a lot of families cannot afford the cost involved in traveling with a sick family member, and patients must travel alone, regardless of their medical condition.

The hospital desperately needed a surgical oncologist with skills like my husband's for many reasons, but especially due to the fact that New Mexico was one of the global hotspots where gallbladder cancer is endemic, nine-fold higher than in non-native population. The reason for this high prevalence is poorly understood and may be related to environmental factors, genetics, or both. Gallbladder cancer is lethal, very aggressive, and can spread quickly, and my husband was particularly qualified to treat the disease.

Our two weeks in Israel were not pleasantly spent. We felt the worst was yet to come. My husband was busy exchanging emails with the NM medical board, his future surgical oncology chief, and the credential department at UNM—the same department that incorrectly approved his credentials at the beginning of the process without noticing he didn't have two years of accredited residency program.

I was busy handling problems regarding the shipment of our belongings from NY to New Mexico—a shipment that might soon need to change direction back to Israel. When the kids asked where they would go to school next year, we truthfully shared we didn't know. After the plane took off from Tel Aviv Ben-Gurion International Airport to the United States, I looked out the window at the Israeli shoreline and whispered, "Goodbye."

21

⚜

GENESIS

On July 19, 2010, we arrived in Albuquerque, New Mexico, and suddenly everything was quiet. We had moved from the city that never sleeps to a city that has real trouble waking up—from a metropolitan area in which you could not see the stars to a place where you could observe each and every constellation. We had replaced the ultimate urban area with a locale for nature lovers. We'd relocated from a place where people want everything yesterday to a place where people actually prefer waiting until tomorrow. This shock therapy is highly recommended to every east-coaster, especially New Yorkers, who could benefit tremendously from living in New Mexico for at least six months of their lives. Nevertheless, for business people, it is the ultimate training for enhancement of cultural skills.

We rented an apartment in one of the many building complexes scattered around Albuquerque. We could not buy or even lease a home without knowing whether we would have to leave soon, or if we could stay. The department of surgery couldn't pay my husband his salary as it was stated by the contract, because he was unable to do the work he was hired to do without a medical license. However, the department chairman understood the seriousness of our situation, and the fact we didn't have any income possibilities, because my visa status restricted me from working. Fortunately, the department paid my husband a small allowance. Our standard of living was very modest, but we still had to give up the idea of having medical insurance.

My husband started studying for the first step of the United States Medical Licensing Examination that measures the way medical school students or graduates can apply key concepts of the sciences fundamental to the practice of medicine. It had been some time since he'd been a medical student, and he had to review much of his learning. At the same time, the university and my husband submitted a petition to change New Mexico's requirements in order to apply for a medical license.

In November, my husband received the score for the step one examination. It was ninety-nine. I believe it was one of those times when the USMLE made sure there wasn't any computer error involved. Later that month, a special assembly of New Mexico's medical board members was scheduled. I couldn't sleep for days prior to this meeting, and throughout the day of the meeting, I couldn't eat anything. My stomach was tense as in an anxiety attack. I wasn't in good shape for almost six months.

At three o'clock in the afternoon of Friday, November 12, 2010, my husband received a phone call. The medical board had accepted the petition, and the two-year accredited residency program requirement would no longer be needed in order to apply for medical licensure in New Mexico. We became an important part of history. We helped to change the status quo, which would not only benefit us, but also the people of New Mexico. The new ruling opened the field to foreign physicians who, unlike American physicians, would be willing to work in the state. Now, New Mexicans would be able to receive quality medical care close to home.

In many hospitals in the United States this requirement still exists, although it is far from being reasonable. I cannot understand why two years of residency in America are more important than two years of a fellowship in America. If anything, two years of advanced training are superior to two years of basic training. Additionally, I am still puzzled by hospitals' requirement for an American board certification. So many highly-qualified foreign physicians who took the same medical licensure examination and have a State's medical license are not welcomed in many hospitals. These hospitals would rather choose a *bored* certified person just because he or she is board-certified, rather than hire an extraordinary physician who is neither.

My husband received his medical license and started building his practice from scratch. Yet, the need for his expertise was so extreme that his operation days were all booked three months in advance, and he had to grab any available OR time to provide care to as many patients as possible. He was the only physician in New Mexico who performed a unique kind of Hepatopancreaticobiliary surgery. The appreciation and gratitude he received from the people of New Mexico and other physicians at the hospital, and in clinics across New Mexico, made him determined to bring state-of-the-art medical care to the Southwest. He also launched research in gallbladder cancer to help understand the reason behind the prevalence of the disease and maybe find ways to prevent the high recurrence in a specific population. Finally, he was appointed to be an advisor to the Navajo nation— a nomination that indicated both trust and respect.

Yet, the kids' schooling was challenging. In 2010, the Quality Counts report ranked New York's overall education system as second in the United States with a B score on students' chance of success. New Mexico's education system was rated in the middle of the table, and second from the bottom on chance of success. Unfortunately, I had to agree with the findings, because a week after the beginning of the school year, I noticed something was very wrong. The problems ranged from the teachers' attitudes towards my son's Dyslexia, to my daughter's second grade English second-language challenges, and to the overall educational culture, which seemed to lack the willingness to adapt advanced teaching methods, or accommodate students' needs in the twenty-first century.

I had to struggle to get a proper evaluation for my fifth grade son, and I advocated for him every step of the way. I researched for available adaptations and literally forced the school to accept and apply them. After a couple of months, I decided the school's experimental time was over, and I searched for a professional Dyslexia therapist who could provide my son with the therapy he needed. I had read about a program that involved the use of visual, auditory, and kinesthetic-tactile pathways simultaneously to enhance memory and learning of written language. The program is called Multisensory Language Training, and it had remarkable results among students with Dyslexia. I contacted the Multisensory Language Training Institute of New Mexico that trains teachers and other education professionals to become Dyslexia therapists and asked for a recommendation for one of their best therapists.

Lucy was a gift from God. She started working with my son four days a week when he was in fifth grade. At the end of the year, I transferred my son from the public system to a charter school. That decision has since proven to be one of the best decisions of my life, and his. The charter school was much-less crowded, the student-teacher ratio was good, and students enjoyed personal instruction. The school was ready to make as many accommodations as were needed to facilitate the education of children with special needs and help them succeed. Instead of having two lessons of associated arts a day, he only had one, and Lucy would work with him during the second period. This was very beneficial, as it allowed my son to receive Dyslexia therapy during the day, instead of after school when he was tired and restless.

In 2011, my son was getting the help he needed; my daughter exhibited a remarkable talent for language and was doing well in school. My husband loved his job, as he felt a sense of mission by providing medical care for people who desperately needed it. And I was home administrating life, but, as much as it was important, that wasn't enough. I wanted more than just to be responsible for everyone's necessities. Since a job wasn't an option, due to the visa restrictions and the market situation in Albuquerque, I finally did what I had wanted to do for years but couldn't. I went back to school.

For the last ten years, I had been fantasizing about a Master's Degree in Business Administration. I had missed education throughout the years, but I could only dream of a master's degree when the children were young or when we lived in Israel. Our financial situation never reached the point where MBA tuition was affordable, and my husband's intense career didn't leave room for a full-time job, let alone advanced education.

Now, I was tired of waiting for the right time. Whenever I read to my children Dr. Seuss' *Oh, The Places You'll Go*, I felt sickened by the number of waiting places. People were "Waiting for a train to go, or a bus to come, or a plane to go, or the mail to come…the phone to ring…waiting around for a yes or no." I had done enough waiting; it was my time, my turn, and my life.

We lived in the United States, my husband's salary was good, and the kids were old enough. I started exploring my options. I could study at the University Of New Mexico School Of Management, or I could find an on-line program somewhere else.

I called the NM management school's advisory line and when the advisor heard my accent, she asked if I was a foreign student. I confirmed that I was, and then she said I would have to take an English proficiency test, submit an income statement, and take a medical exam. I figured this probably would not be the type of school I was looking for.

The next stop was Northeastern University that was located in Boston and had a great reputation for its online MBA program. When I called the admission office, the advisor was interested in my background and my previous education. She asked for three recommendation letters, and a transcript from the university I had previously attended. It took me a couple of weeks to gather the required information and send it back to the administration office. I received a call the next day; the advisor said Northeastern University would be honored to have me as an MBA student.

I HAD MADE IT. I had finally made it. I was excited, happy, and motivated. Finally, once again, after a very long time, I was in first place. At long last it was again about me, my aspirations, my goals, my wants. I could not wait for the first day of school. I felt the need to learn, expand my horizons, and become familiar with the American business world. I had traveled and worked with people from around the world, but the MBA was the link to the American culture of which I had become a part. I felt that being a working professional in America required me to know the history of American industry, and to understand American firms' state-of-mind. If I wanted to be a successful employee or entrepreneur, the MBA would be a great start.

In hindsight, I didn't have a clue what I was up against. The MBA program turned out to be the most challenging thing I had ever experienced, and it was for a good reason. During my last year in the program, Northeastern University's online MBA program was ranked number one in the United States and number three globally in the Financial Times 2014 inaugural ranking of online MBA programs.

22

PERSEVERANCE

*I*n August 2011, our request for a change in visa status from extraordinary, O visa, to foreign worker in specialty occupations, H visa, was approved, and the stopwatch of three years' service in a medically underserved area was started. Once again, we needed to commute all the way to the American consulate in Israel to change the status of our passports. Upon our return, the lawyer started gathering the documentation needed for the permanent residency application. Even if our application were approved, we would be unable to receive a green card, and I would be unable to work until our three years in an underserved area came to an end.

Once again, life was busy, hectic, and full to the limit, and I loved every minute of it. I started my online MBA at Northeastern University as any other American student. There were available programs for foreign and international students, but I didn't feel a need to apply for any of them. I was on my way to becoming an American employee in America, not a foreign employee in America, and because I didn't want any special treatment at my future workplace, I was determined not to receive any accommodations during my studies.

My first MBA course was Ethics in Workplace, which proved to be extremely relevant for any employee, because it analyzed topics such as implicit prejudice, in-group favoritism, and over-claiming of credit. Throughout my years as a business graduate, on top of the scholarly articles, academic textbooks, and media data, I read *The Wall Street Journal* daily, and was a subscriber of the *Bloomberg Businessweek*. If I had to name one topic that should continuously be discussed in the industry, politics, K-12 education, and elsewhere, it would be ethics, because judging from my experience, America is far from where it probably wants to be or should be when it comes to ethics.

Ethics in the work place goes far beyond implicit or explicit prejudice. Lack of moral philosophy was responsible for the 2008 financial crisis, the demise of companies such as Enron and WorldCom, and was apparent when bonuses were given to AIG's executives immediately after the company received a tax-payer bailout.

Today more explicitly than ever, the police force, which enforces the law and protects order, is being accused of prejudgment and racial profiling. Corporate America is blamed for being biased against minorities such as women, people of color, and immigrants. The National Security Agency redefines American and international civil liberties without addressing their actions or providing an explanation regarding the invasion of privacy they inflict on the innocents they're protecting. In schools, educators serve as role models, but many times they fail to recognize their professional image is impacted by their conduct both on and, more importantly, off the job. Our society is quick to judge, form opinions based on stereotypes, and promote superficiality.

The course in ethics touched many aspects of life and opened my eyes to a subject that we all think we understand, but fail to follow. It was also an introduction to my MBA studies. I struggled with the textbooks, articles, the online discussions, and lectures. For the first time in my life, I studied in English. Suddenly, I was able to relate to the difficulties my children were experiencing. Acquiring education in a foreign language is challenging, and adjusting to the amount of reading and writing is equally difficult. After the second course, I asked Lucy, my son's Dyslexia teacher, for private lessons in English, so I could submit professionally written assignments. We worked together over the course of one year, after which my assignments reached English language proficiency.

I stretched my MBA program to almost three years, because I wanted to spend time with my kids during the summer break, which lasts close to three months in New Mexico. During the rest of the year, I was fully committed to my studies. I was determined to make the best out of this amazing opportunity to gain knowledge, as knowledge is one of the few things that can never be overvalued. During this time, my children were exposed to the challenges I had to overcome, the motivation I needed to sustain throughout my studies, and the small victories I worked incredibly hard to attain.

A good role model should talk the talk, and walk the walk, and I was fortunate enough to pass down to my children my mother's heritage, which she had bestowed upon me. She had raised me to believe education is always relevant, and always worthwhile. My mom said that who you are is what you've learned, and the more knowledge one absorbs, the better person he or she becomes. Mother has never stopped studying, and from my childhood until today, I still watch her learn. There should never be a limit to how much education one can acquire, or how much knowledge one can attain. Access to education should become available to everyone from preschool, through elementary, and high school, and even college.

By enrolling in an MBA program in my forties, not only have I gained valuable comprehension, but I have provided a personal example to my children, and showed them that perseverance is the matter from which dreams come true.

Our family has evolved significantly during the last six years. In our household, two cultures reside in peace and fructify each other. My husband and I are Israelis, and our children are totally American. This fact couldn't have been clearer when on a Sunday morning we overheard the kids arguing about something.

Our daughter sternly demanded, "Give it to me, or I will not speak to you again."

Our son nonchalantly replied, "Well, you do have the right to remain silent..."

She irately blurted, "And you have the right to remain stupid."

To which he firmly uttered, "Be quiet, or you'll get a cruel and unusual punishment."

She stormed into the living room and cried, "He's abusing the Bill of Rights." Indeed, they are American children.

The differences between our cultures are noticeable; we behave, think, and speak differently. We have been teaching each other so many things about our cultures. The contribution to the knowledge reservoir is bidirectional, and it is an amazing experience to learn from children. We save our traditions and cherish our past, while we adapt and adjust to our permanent culture. We light Hanukkah candles in red, blue, and white. We celebrate Thanksgiving with our American friends. We share with our children the events that are happening in Israel, and we all watch the State Of The Union address, and the presidential debates.

My daughter often looks at me in disbelief when I fail to call things by their proper names. Recently, I asked her why she was wearing a hat around the house, and she explained it was a beanie, and when I expressed my opinion about the half-shirt she was wearing, she said it was a crop-top and advised me to expand my "Vogue-cabulary."

My son expresses great disappointment in my husband's lack of knowledge of football or hockey. He was horrified when I prepared finger sandwiches and mini-fruit cakes for a Super Bowl party he held for his friends. Instead, I had to pick up chicken wings from KFC and stop by the grocery store for chips, salsa, guacamole, and spinach dip.

Becoming immigrants in the United States has influenced our entire existence. Imagine that like a child you need to learn new things about your world. You need to learn social codes, language, and new places. We are constantly stimulated and challenged by our ecosystem. We haven't been bored for many years, because we are continuously facing a wide range of challenges. Every day we learn new words or phrases, codes of conducts, rules, and regulations from every aspect of life. When your brain is constantly stimulated, and you are regularly busy with conquering new peaks, you feel vital and you feel young.

Each year, we travel to places we have never been before. We have visited more than twenty-five states so far and have pretty much covered the national parks out west. Last summer, we stood atop Pikes Peak and looked around us with astonishment and read from the monument, Katharine Lee Bates' poem "America the Beautiful." It was a special moment we will all remember forever.

The last four years in New Mexico have taught me so many things about both America and myself. New Mexico is a unique place and very different than any of the coastal states. It is culturally diverse; however, it has been unable to leverage its diversity to achieve significant development and growth, as other states in the area have done. If I had been given a choice of where to live in America, I would probably have chosen New York. But then I would never have known the best sunsets in the world are located 2,000 miles west, and that you can actually hear silence and taste clouds. I would never have known that the funniest bird in the world prefers running on roads over flying, that there are many different kinds of horses, and that the Hatch green chile growing along the Hatch Valley of the Rio Grande is matchless.

When I first heard we would have to live in an underserved area for three years, I thought it was going to be a huge compromise, but I was willing to accept it, because it was the only option available if we wanted to emigrate to the United States. In retrospect, living out of my comfort zone was the most enriching experience I have ever had. When I am able to choose where to live in the United States, I am not sure where I will go, but most of my decision will be based on facts and experience, rather than on assumptions or stereotypes.

On September 12, 2012, I was driving home after picking up the kids from school when my husband called. "Hey, hon, the attorney just called, and our permanent residency was approved, we will be able to submit out permanent residency application in two years." He sounded so excited.

I stopped the car on the side of the road, turned around to the kids, laughed through tears, and told them, "Guys, we've made it. We were approved for a green card; we are welcome to stay in America."

The time had passed quickly, and we were building a future in the United States. My husband was establishing his clinic, the kids were doing great in school, and I was studying intensely for my MBA. In April 2012, the attorney had gathered all the documents required for the permanent residency petition that she intended to submit on September 1st.

On May 12, 2014, we attended the medical exam that green card applicants must undergo. At the clinic, the nurse reviewed our immunization records, and concluded we would need to be vaccinated against diseases that we had never had nor had at the time. After she took samples of blood for testing, I entered the civil surgeon's office, and he asked me health-related questions.

"I now need to check for skin problems, so I'll leave the room while you take off all of your clothing and lay on the table," he instructed.

"I've lived in the Unites States seven years," I stated. "You've approved my immunization record; I'm from one of the most westernized countries in the world. Is this really necessary?" I moved uncomfortably in my seat.

He didn't look at me. "The purpose of the examination is to ensure an applicant is not inadmissible to the U.S. on public health grounds." He snapped. "If you want to become a citizen of the United States, I suggest you start by taking off your clothes."

I slowly took off my white linen dress and carefully folded it on the chair. I thought about the irony of the situation. During the last thirteen years, I had voluntarily exposed myself emotionally and cerebrally to life's multifaceted situations, yet this physical exposure was rattling me in a way I had never felt before.

Lying naked on the cold table, I closed my eyes and listened to my husband talking to our children while waiting for his medical examination. America was right: my husband was extraordinary. He was the only physician in New Mexico who performed unique kinds of liver, pancreas, bile duct, and gallbladder surgeries. Over the past four years, he had introduced new modalities of therapy that were only available in leading cancer centers across the United States. Physicians in the four corners area had become familiar with his practice, and he had provided services to patients from New Mexico, Utah, Arizona, Texas, west Oklahoma, and southern Colorado. He took cases that leading institutions would not take, because they were considered too risky and could influence the hospital's financial bottom-line or their reputation. He saved people's lives every day, yet he was humble, questioned himself all the time, and never let us forget that living a life without making any contribution was like not having lived at all.

23

IF YOU DARE TO DREAM

On August 28th, 2014, we traveled to Boston for my MBA graduation ceremony. I had finished with honors and a dual specialization in marketing and international management. My parents were there together with my husband and our children, and when I was invited to the stage to accept my degree, I felt as if my heart was about to explode with pride. It was by far the greatest self-improvement journey I could ever have taken. On that stage, I was credited for my personal accomplishment.

This achievement was only designed for me. The fact I studied for the MBA in my forties contributed significantly to my successes. I had more than twelve years' experience in the industry, during which I had acted based on my intuition and common sense. I had gained success, but I had also made mistakes. My Master's in Business Administration provided me with an opportunity to reflect back and assess some of the decisions I had made, and to pat myself on the shoulder for the achievements I had accomplished. The MBA reminded me that experience is important, but without education, something would always be missing. It was like trying to build a blockhouse without using mortar; you would get a structure, but it would never be complete.

Immigration to America was a life-changing decision and probably the hardest decision we've made. The emotional and mental price tag attached to it was beyond expensive, but we were willing to pay it for a better future. Even in today's global village when people often become expatriates, relocate, go offshore, or simply move away, leaving your birth country is an exceptionally hard decision. For us, becoming American citizens means we accept citizens' rights and responsibilities that go far beyond voting or running for federal office. It means we pledge our allegiance to America and to what it stands for. We are immigrants, neither guests nor visitors, thus the future of America is entwined with ours, and we will contribute whatever we can to help America succeed. We will always care for our native land, but we are committed to our homeland.

Throughout my journey, I have experienced a fair share of conflict and pain. Nothing was easy, or taken for granted, and everything was a struggle. I have struggled to find solutions to impossible situations. I had to make unpopular and uncomfortable compromises, and trade what was best for my family with what was best for me.

My life-altering experience involved immigration, but it could have easily been interchangeable with any other unexpected circumstance such as losing a loved one, losing a job, having a baby in a later phase in life, or having to care for a sick family member. No matter what prompts the need to shake a life, it is always possible to reposition or rejuvenate yourself. Yet, I learned the ability to succeed is strongly and positively correlated with the ability to overlook every concept you lived by that cannot fit into your new reality.

My breakthrough was when I discovered I could outsmart feminism. I understood that feminism is anything but one-size-fits-all, and women have infinite routes of self-expression. A woman's essence is not necessarily related to her career, her family, her education, her connections, or her hobbies. A woman's true spirit is in her ability to make the choices that are right for her, given the reality she faces, and according to her personal preferences.

Had I insisted to hold the feminist values I lived by in my early thirties, I would have felt I had given up, that I had failed, and I would have lived with

196 | SHARON NIR

a constant feeling of disappointment in myself for not following the route I had set for myself when I was in my early twenties. However, I succeeded to put aside my naïve concepts, focus on the reality I faced, and make the unpopular decision to promote my family over myself. Yet, I found that what was best for my family, eventually proved to be best for me, as well. I proved I can be the woman I always wanted to be. I have no regrets over the loss of my career. On the contrary, I have supported and accompanied my husband and my children during the years they needed me the most. At times, my entire family leaned on me, and I had the strength to carry on.

After so many years, I am where I want to be and can do whatever I like. My children are grown, my husband is doing what he loves, and I have years of business experience with an MBA to back it up. Soon I will be able to go back to work and ignite my career. It was worth it; it was all worth it.

On a February Tuesday evening, when New Mexico's skies flaunted one of its most glorious lava sunsets, I collected the mail from our mailbox. There were four nondescript envelopes and in them were our green cards. It was the first day of the rest of my life, and the horizon couldn't have been brighter.

END

CPSIA information can be obtained
at www.ICGtesting.com
Printed in the USA
FSOW04n1411190216
17130FS